Transport to Disaster

JAMES W. ELLIOTT

Transport
to
Disaster

NEW YORK

HOLT, RINEHART AND WINSTON

Designer: Ernst Reichl

82334–0112

Printed in the United States of
America

To the memory of my father,
Green Smith Elliott,
who first told me the story.

Contents

Transport to Disaster

≈ I ≈

Messenger of
Death

At the Cincinnati construction yard where the boat
was built, a workman painted seven letters, black and
bold, across each of her paddle-wheel housings. *Sultana* she was called, after a royal consort or favored
concubine of an Oriental potentate. Her designer,
Captain Preston Lodwick, had chosen the fanciful
name out of pride in her grace and beauty, and at the
launching, on February 4, 1863, observers agreed that
the craft was worthy of her name. Yet this regally titled
steamer, in spite of her obvious charms, was destined
to achieve a macabre distinction. For one night, just as
the Civil War was drawing to a close, she became the
central figure in the greatest marine disaster of all
time.

3

Up in the broad-windowed pilothouse, George Clayton cramped the wheel hard over. Majestically the *Sultana* swung in a lazy arc, her side paddles slapping a staccato rhythm in the muddy water of the Mississippi River. With precision, the pilot twirled the spokes back in a blur of motion, expertly meeting the *Sultana*'s movement as she took a proper heading. Then, by three measured tugs at the bell rope, he gave the landing signal. It was late afternoon, almost sundown, when the handsome white packet tied up alongside the wharf at Cairo, Illinois. The day was Good Friday, April 14, 1865.

Half a continent away, the streets of Washington were dark and Abraham Lincoln was working at his desk in the Executive Mansion. In two hours, the President would walk into Ford's Theater on Tenth Street. In three hours, he would be carried from the theater with a derringer ball in his brain. In twelve hours, he would be dead.

Tomorrow's newspapers would be bordered in black, but today's were crammed with good news for Northern readers. The war was almost over. LEE SURRENDERS TO GRANT, the headlines had trumpeted only five days before, and now Sherman was ready to gather up Joe Johnston and the last ragged Rebel army. The back pages were still burdened with long casualty lists, and according to front-page advertisements, the Waters Publishing Company of Broadway was doing a brisk business in a song called, "Oh! Send Me One Rose from His Grave." But the "classification" columns also offered more hopeful fare. For thirty cents a copy, the reader could buy such topical tunes as "Richmond Is

Ours," by Mrs. E. A. Parkhurst, or "General Sherman's Triumphal March," by G. C. Norman.

At Cairo, now that the war was ending, the front pages were carrying an increasing number of steamboat notices. The *Sultana*'s announcement read:

> The regular and unsurpassed passenger packet "Sultana," in command of Capt. J. Cass Mason, departs tomorrow morning at 10 o'clock for New Orleans, Memphis and all way landings. The "Sultana" is a good boat, as well as a fleet one. Mr. Wm. Gamble has control of the office affairs, while our friends Thomas McGinty and James O'Hara will be found in the saloon, where everything of the "spirit" order can be had in due time.

The *Sultana* had left St. Louis on Thursday night, dropping down between the rolling, spring-clad hills of Missouri and Illinois; past the old French settlements of Ste. Genevieve and Kaskaskia; by Grand Tower, which took its name from a huge pillar of rock standing out of the swirling tide; through the chute at Cape Girardeau; around Steersman's Bend where the channel was deep; from Thebes to Commerce along the Grand Chain, a string of sunken stones that could cripple and kill; beside the forested splotches of Goose Island, Jacket Pattern and the Two Sisters; and at last to the southern border of Illinois.

Traffic on the Upper River, although far below the volume of prewar days, had been heavy, and the *Sultana* had met several other steamers along the way. Most of the old packets were gone, scuttled by their

Southern owners to prevent capture, or sunk in battle by one side or the other. But now that the few survivors had been reinforced by new construction, dozens of side-wheelers were once more to be seen on the Mississippi.

At sunset on this Good Friday there was nothing uncommon about the *Sultana* and her journey from St. Louis to New Orleans; just as there was nothing extraordinary about Ford's Theater and its production of "Our American Cousin." It was death which would make them memorable.

The dawn of Saturday broke bright and clear at Cairo, promising a beautiful spring day. Then, shortly after sunrise, a chattering telegraph wire brought the ugly news that was spreading, as Ralph Waldo Emerson saw it, "like the shadow of an uncalculated eclipse over the planet." The message from Washington, signed by Edwin M. Stanton, Secretary of War, contained one terse sentence: "Abraham Lincoln died this morning at 22 minutes after 7 o'clock."

Quick-fingered printers at the Cairo *War Eagle* used their biggest type to set the headline,

NATIONAL CALAMITY

and the death notice was followed by the text of a previous dispatch: "Last evening, about 10:30 P.M., at Ford's Theater, the president, while sitting in his private box with Mrs. Lincoln, Miss Harris, and Major Rathbone, was shot by an assassin, who suddenly entered the box and approached behind the president. The assassin then leaped upon the stage, brandishing a large dagger or knife, and made his escape in the rear of the theater. The pistol ball entered the back of the president's head, and penetrated nearly through the head. The wound is mortal. The president has been insensible ever since it was inflicted, and is now dying."

Extras were on the streets before breakfast. And, as it was later chronicled by the New York *Herald,* "From one member of the family to the other, from room to room, and up and down every stairway, this awful piece of news was reported, and stunned and paralyzed everyone. And it was a natural tribute to the position held by this great man in the hearts of the people that if it had been the dearest member of each of those households that had been stricken down the sudden horror and anguish could hardly have been greater."

Cairo reacted like hundreds of other towns and villages across the nation. Small knots of mourners talked in hushed tones, or simply stood quietly together, their grief beyond words. Storekeepers hung hand-lettered signs in their windows—Closed for the Day—and walked home with tears rolling down their cheeks. Church bells filled the air and their clamorous dirge was punctuated every half hour by the rolling crash of cannon.

Upstate, in Coles County, Illinois, farm neighbors carried the sad tidings to Lincoln's stepmother, Sally Bush. The old woman stood in the doorway, listened stoically and then said, "I knowed when he went away that he'd never come back."

Secretary of War Stanton had ordered that the news be withheld from all of the military districts of the

South, and almost a month would pass before Atlanta and Mobile and other isolated cities learned that the President had been shot. But it would take more than an order from Stanton to keep such a secret bottled up at Cairo. The tragic report was certain to move downriver with the first steamboat, and the *Sultana* was already billowing smoke and raising pressure.

There was a delay, of course. Due to the sorrow and excitement, the impatient packet did not leave "on the advertised" at ten o'clock. By midafternoon, however, Captain Mason had her away from the landing and into the channel, chopping along through the rich tobacco region of Kentucky.

Edward Ingram, the second pilot, was now at the wheel, spinning the spokes with practiced ease and feeling the usual sense of relief at "getting out of the river"—the southbound pilot's term for clearing Cairo and putting astern the rock-bottomed Upper River, where the steamboat wrecks were said to average one for every mile. Out ahead of the packet's pointed bow stretched the broader, deeper Lower River, which was really a different kind of stream altogether.

For the Father of Waters, as Ingram well knew, has a different character for every clime. Trickling out of Lake Itasca, Minnesota, bounding away between banks that are dotted with reeds and water grass, he is a placid Yankee with faultless manners. But just above St. Louis, eleven hundred miles from his birthplace, he is doubled in size by the red-complected Missouri and becomes a rowdy Midwestern roughneck. Then at Cairo, after another two hundred miles, his size is almost doubled again by the torrent of the Ohio, and he is ready to sweep into Dixie as the irascible Old Man of legend and song.

Less than three hours after leaving Cairo, the *Sultana* steamed past Columbus, Kentucky, and on into the gathering night. Through the black hours, guided by that magical instinct known only to migrant birds and steamboat pilots, she followed the fickle ribbon of water. Weaving her way among the islands numbered eight to twenty-one, she winked her lamplights at New Madrid, Missouri, swung around Plumb Point and Craig-head's Point, scurried under the friendly but fearsome guns of Fort Pillow and met the morning at the head of Island 37, by Brandywine Bar.

Memphis hove into view before noon on Easter Sunday, and the city's wharf was drowsing in unaccustomed quiet until the *Sultana's* gangplank rattled into place. Moments later came the explosion of alarm and near panic. There were running feet and shouts. "President Lincoln is dead!" Clusters of men and women struggled and stretched for a glance at the precious copies of the Cairo *War Eagle*. Haltingly the words were read aloud, slowly, painfully: "Abraham Lincoln died this morning at 22 minutes after 7 o'clock . . . shot by an assassin." The same scene was repeated the next day when Helena, Arkansas, learned of what General Joseph Johnston was to call, "the greatest possible calamity to the South." Gone was the man who had hoped to end the war without bitterness, "With malice toward none; with charity for all." In his place was one who had spoken ominously of traitors and had declared, "Their reward should be the halter and the gallows." Little wonder that somber dread and dark foreboding followed the *Sultana* as she carried the news of the assassination to all of the cities and towns along the Lower River.

On Tuesday the *Sultana* stopped at Lake Providence, Louisiana, and then glided down into the "voodoo lan'" of the Deep South's swamps and canebrakes. The April sun was summer-hot, and there was a sticky, tropical swelter in the air. As the morning wore on, passengers deserted their staterooms to look for a breeze on deck. After lunch they hurried back to the rails to compete for a first glimpse of the hill cities which sprang up out of the dense, verdant lowland.

Vicksburg, high and haughty, stood at the tip of a twelve-mile hairpin curve. In spite of its elevation, the city could not be seen until the packet rounded into the turn. Then suddenly it loomed ahead, a grim-visaged cliff with a thatch of rooftops on its craggy brow and with its chin resting on a narrow steamboat landing. Mutilated trees, earthworks and shell craters were reminders of the forty-seven-day siege that had at last unlocked the citadel to Union forces after every plan of direct attack had failed. Boasting a north-south river and an east-west railroad, the former Gibraltar of the Confederacy was now an important terminal point for the shipment of Federal troops and supplies.

Downstream at Natchez, under the bluffs, straggled the shabby spit of land that had once been the toughest town on the Mississippi. Now almost deserted, a scattering of tumbled-down shacks was all that remained of the one-time brawling, bawdy port where Mike Fink and his fellows had gambled and fought during the rugged flatboat era. Long before the steamboat made its appearance, and for a number of years after, Natchez-under-the-Hill had been a popular stopover for the traders, farmers and trappers who came swarming downriver on their log rafts and keelboats. This eroded strip had been lively enough in those days, and deadly enough, too. Natchez-on-the-Hill, the beautiful city atop the bluffs, had lost much of its former gaiety, but little of its fabled charm. It was still the storybook town of imposing mansions, embowered with massive magnolia trees and perfumed with the heady fragrance of their giant blossoms.

It was on the Natchez bluffs in 1812 that an aged Negro, watching the *New Orleans*, the first Mississippi steamboat, come splashing by, had tossed his hat to the sky and whooped, "Ole Mississippi done met her massa now!"

The first lady of the river was quickly followed by others of her kind—the *Vesuvius*, the *Aetna*, the *Buffalo*—all built by Robert Fulton and Robert R. Livingston, the same men who had designed and financed the original. Three decades after the maiden voyage of the *New Orleans*, the river was crowded with steamboats. An official list issued in January, 1834, gave a total of two hundred and thirty, and a few years later the number had doubled. By 1853, there were forty-one lines with headquarters in New Orleans; no less than three thousand three hundred and seven arrivals were reported at St. Louis in a single year; and steamboating was in its rollicking heyday.

Just as 1811 marked the origin of the Mississippi steamboat species, so 1850 marked the end of its evolution. After that time, there were no important changes in structure or appearance. Every feature of the imposing creature had been born of necessity or convenience. Each part had a purpose and was strategically located to serve that purpose to best advantage. The tall jack staff on the forecastle was there so the pilot could sight his course as a hunter aims his rifle. A builder named Billy King had noticed that the bow wave plunged low in the middle section of the boat, so the paddle wheels had been moved aft of amidships to catch the bow wave on its second rise. Aside from its engines, the river steamer was purebred American and unlike anything else in the world.

The *Sultana* was an outstanding specimen—a harmonious mélange of paddle wheels and people—a model Mississippi steamer with the customary, colorful crew. She was a Lodwick boat, built for Captain Preston Lodwick, which is to say that she was several cuts above the average. Lodwick had won considerable renown as a construction superintendent at the Cincinnati yards, where he had helped design and produce such superior packets as the *Northern Belle,* the *Northern Light* and the *Prince of Wales.* And when his crowning achievement, the *Sultana,* dropped down to the Ohio River levee on February 4, 1863, to receive her first cargo for Pittsburgh, the Cincinnati *Daily Commercial* declared her to be "one of the largest and best business steamers ever constructed." Registered at seven hundred and nineteen tons, she was rated at one thousand tons capacity. Yet in spite of her size and weight, she walked the water like a lady, trimming on a draft of just thirty-four inches. Her construction cost was sixty thousand dollars, and she was licensed to carry seventy-six cabin passengers and three hundred deck passengers and crewmen.

From stem to stern the *Sultana* measured two hundred and sixty feet, and her other vital statistics were equally impressive—a beam of forty-two feet, a maximum deck width of thirty-nine feet and a hold seven feet deep. The hull, flat-bottomed and shallow, with its pencil-thin length-to-width ratio of better than six to one, was fragile and ill-proportioned by ocean-going standards, but it was ideally suited to negotiating chutes and sand bars along the less violent inland waterways. Each end of this hollow foundation was punctured by a cargo hatch, and at its center were arrayed the fuel bins, boilers and engines, partially surrounded by a wooden bulkhead to protect the crew from wind and weather.

Up until about 1850 all steamboats were wood-burners, and it was necessary for the pilot to pull into the bank every few miles to "wood the boat" at one of the scores of woodyards which lined the forest's edge. After a decade of transition, however, most of the packets had been converted to coal-burning boilers, which allowed them to make the St. Louis to New Orleans run with only one or two refueling stops. Even into the 70's there were still a number of wood-burners on the river, operated by captains who preferred to move a little slower and, by the same token, stay a great deal cleaner. But the majority, Captain Lodwick among them, accepted soot as the unavoidable price of progress. The *Sultana's* four high-pressure boilers, horizontal tanks forty-six inches in diameter and eighteen feet long, were of the coal-burning type.

13

Her engines, with cylinders twenty-five inches in diameter and eight feet strokes, worked a pair of side wheels which measured thirty-four feet in diameter and carried eight-foot buckets.

Near the forecastle, a wide stairway wound up to the *Sultana's* boiler deck. Actually this second level of the boat was misnamed, since it was intended for the accommodation of passengers, not boilers. Beginning flush with its after edge and reaching almost to the head of the stairway was the tunnel-like cabin, or saloon, strung with glittering glass chandeliers, embellished with yard on yard of gilded jigsaw work, and otherwise decorated in accordance with the Victorian notion of luxury and elegance. An ornate bar, fully stocked and highly polished, stood against the forward wall, hemmed in by a friendly semicircle of small tables. Far away from this tipler's haven, a fifty-foot portion of the after section was partitioned off and richly carpeted to provide a somewhat secluded ladies' cabin.

Both sides of the *Sultana's* cavernous social hall were lined with doors, every one adorned with a porcelain knob and a distinctive oil painting. Behind each door was a stateroom—a tiny cubical furnished with a double-deck bunk. The accommodations for ladies were eight feet square, while the others were somewhat smaller.

One traveler who shared such a compartment with her sister on the *Grey Eagle* reported: "In the stateroom, where we had to sleep and dress and, if we could snatch a chance, take an afternoon nap, there was a corner shelf for a basin and pitcher, and one chair; two doors, one leading out (to the boiler deck) and the other leading in (to the cabin), transoms over each for light and ventilation—and there you are for over a week." Quite naturally, the lady fails to mention one inevitable and indispensable item—the chamberpot.

Their staterooms might have been cramped in size, but in all other respects the *Sultana's* cabin passengers were the pampered beneficiaries of a highly competitive business. Delicate china decorated the long collapsible table which was set up in the main cabin at mealtimes. Food was of a quality and quantity that could hardly fail to delight the most exacting gourmet or satisfy the most ravenous trencherman. Between feasts there was a choice of convivial card-playing and drinking in the main saloon or polite conversation in the ladies' cabin. For those made lethargic by overindulgence, the boiler-deck promenade offered fresh air and ever-changing scenery, plus an abundance of Windsor armchairs and shiny brass cuspidors.

Negroes and the less prosperous whites traveled as deck passengers, a status roughly equivalent to "steerage" on a salt-water vessel. Confined to the main deck along with the crew, the freight and the boilers, they ate from tin plates and slept on the bare planks.

Above the cabin was the hurricane deck, also called the promenade deck. At its after verge hung the yawl, a small rowboat which could be sent ahead of the steamer with a lead-line, to test the water's depth when the pilot was feeling his way over a sand bar. And rising from the middle of this third level was a small cabin—the texas—which provided private quarters for the boat's officers, with the captain's drawing room occupying the forward end.

The officers' quarters were called the "texas" because one steamboat's rooms had been named for the states of the Union and passengers were assigned accordingly: "Boy, take this gentleman's bags to the Alabama room!" The names, of course, were painted on the doors, and there were enough doors to honor every state except Texas, which had just been admitted. To make up for the omission, the cabin on top of the boat was dubbed the texas, and the name stuck.

High over all, on the texas roof, at the pinnacle of the boat, roosted the pilothouse, ringed with glass windows. Its interior was dominated by the big spoked wheel, standing five feet or more in height. Overhead dangled a plaited rope, leading to the steam whistle, and a cord which reached down to the brass bell on the hurricane deck. Across one side of the room stretched a long bench where visitors could sit and gossip. On most of the more luxurious boats, such as the *Sultana*, the bench was flanked by gleaming spittoons, and the deck was covered with oilcloth.

All things considered, the construction yards, with their hand tools and resinous pine timbers, turned out a better product than anyone had a right to expect. Steamboats, however, were not built to last. Their average life span was only four or five years, and their crude boilers were as dangerous as ticking time bombs.

Henry Shreve's *George Washington*, the tenth vessel to be constructed for the Mississippi trade, was the first to blow up, killing thirteen crewmen in June,

1816, and setting a deadly example. By 1860, almost two hundred floating palaces had been destroyed by boiler explosions, and more than fifteen hundred persons had been crushed, scalded and burned to death, or mercifully drowned, as a result. The perils of navigation—snags, rocks and collisions—also took their toll, and fire was an ever-present danger. But the most dreaded cry on the river was, "The boilers have burst!"

When the *Louisiana* let go at the crowded New Orleans levee, one hundred and fifty died, and the city was given a harrowing demonstration of the destructive power of steam. *Lloyd's Directory* matter-of-factly recorded the terrifying event:

"A few minutes after five o'clock on the evening of November 15, 1849, the steamboat *Louisiana*, Captain Cannon, lying at the foot of Gravier Street, New Orleans, had completed all the preparations for her departure for St. Louis. She was laden with a valuable cargo, and had on board a large number of passengers. The last bell was rung, and the machinery set in motion; but at the moment the boat disengaged herself from the wharf and began to back out into the river, all the boilers exploded with a concussion which shook all the houses for many squares around to their very foundations. The *Louisiana* was lying between two other steamers—the *Bostonia* and *Storm*—the upper works of which were completely wrecked; their chimneys were carried away, and their cabins were shattered to small fragments. The violence of the explosion was such that large pieces of the boilers were blown hundreds of yards from the wharf, falling on the levee and in different parts of the city. One of these iron fragments cut a mule in two, and then struck a horse and dray, killing both driver and horse instantly. Another mass of iron, of considerable size, was projected to the corner of Canal and Front Streets, two hundred yards from the exploded steamer, where it threw down three large iron pillars which supported the roof of a coffee house. Before it reached the iron pillars, this fragment passed through several bales of cotton which lay in its passage."

The *Louisiana* disaster, like all the others, was followed by an uproar of indignation and demands that something be done to stop the carnage. For a time there was even a movement to outlaw the high-pressure engine, but nothing came of it. The people of this reckless and romantic age were more concerned with speed and elegance than with safety and durability, and the builders, including Captain Lodwick, gave them what they wanted.

Of all the Lodwick boats, the *Sultana* proved to be the most successful. In a single year of operation, she netted her designer better than twice her original cost, and early in 1864, deciding to retire with his profits, he sold her to Captain J. Cass Mason and five associates for a reported eighty thousand dollars. Mason took a one-sixteenth interest; Nanson, Dameron and Company, three-eighths; William A. Thornburg, one-quarter; Samuel DeBow and Company, one-eighth; William J. Gamble, one-eighth; and William Sands, one-sixteenth.

By dint of hard work, and to a lesser degree by virtue of a fortunate marriage, Captain Mason had climbed

the ladder of steamboat success. A native of Lynch-
burg, Virginia, he had been brought to the banks of
the Missouri as a child, had caught paddle-wheel fever
at an early age and had spent his working life on the
riverboats, serving as clerk of the *Herald,* the *William
Campbell* and the *A. B. Chambers,* among others.

In 1860, he married Rowena Dozier of Dozier's
Landing, a sprawling estate on the Missouri riverside
near St. Louis, and thus became a son-in-law of Captain James Dozier, one of the titans of steamboating.
Captain Jim had nine sons and daughters, and so many
packets it was hard to keep count—the *Warsaw,* the
Lake of the Woods, the *St. Louis Oak,* the *Cora,* the
Mary Blane, the *Elvira,* the *Thomas E. Tutt* and
the *Mollie Dozier,* to mention a few.

Although the Masons' only child died in infancy,
the marriage was a happy one. Because her husband
was most often on the river, Rowena continued to live
at the family home, and Mason soon found himself
installed as commander of a fine new Dozier packet
named, with paternal pride, the *Rowena.* But soon
Captain Mason tired of living in the shadow of his
illustrious father-in-law and in the spring of '63 Mason
moved into the St. Louis to New Orleans trade as
master of the *Belle Memphis,* a first-class boat, and
one which did not display the Dozier monogram on
her dinner plates.

By the time he took his place in the *Sultana's* texas,
Mason was thirty-four years old and had won the
warm respect of his colleagues and competitors. "A
sharp man with a boat," they called him—the highest
compliment. He was also described as a "steady and

19

reliable gentleman" and was given a reputation for being "decided, firm and conscientious" by those who knew him well.

If an ideal master could have been built, part on part, like a steamboat, Mason might have served as a pattern. Five-ten in height, he was spare of build and fair-complected, with sandy whiskers and mustache—young enough, tall enough, lean enough and bearded enough to cut a handsome figure in his black frock coat, the uniform of his calling.

As general manager of the boat, he was necessarily much concerned with his customers—courting favor with the important shippers, welcoming passengers, settling disagreements and charming the ladies. By the nature of riverboat travel, of course, he was denied the rigid authority of a sea captain. But he was, nevertheless, responsible for everything and everyone on board.

From the texas above to the fires down below, Captain Cass Mason was king of the *Sultana*, but he had little control over George J. Clayton and Edward Ingram, the lords of the pilothouse. These Mississippi River pilots were a power unto themselves, keeping their own counsel and taking orders from no one in matters of boat handling. They were hired by the captain, but once the steamer left the wharf, their power over navigation was absolute. No captain would dare to question the judgment of his pilots. The respect that they commanded was well earned, for they had to know every twist, bend, bottom and bulge in the stream. At all hours, in fair weather and foul, the boat's safety depended upon the pilot's uncanny ability to find a clear passage along twelve or thirteen hundred miles of restless, shifting river, without the guidance of a single lighthouse or channel marker.

Among the most arduous jobs aboard the *Sultana* were those of William Rowberry and William Butler, the first and second mates, who served as deck foreman and cargo boss. Getting a full day's work out of the hard-bitten deck hands and carefree Negro roustabouts was no easy task. It required a large measure of understanding and no inconsiderable amount of cursing. Typically, the steamboat mate was big and burly, whiskered and tattooed, and he attacked his sundry problems with a raging gusto which was awesome to behold. Even his smallest command was delivered in an angry roar, and his every "heave" and "belay" was accompanied by a sulfurous stream of profanity.

Between them, the chief engineer, Nathan Wintrenger, and his assistant, Wes Clemens, were responsible for the *Sultana's* boilers and engines. Together they ruled the dirty and dangerous domain of sweating stokers, roaring fireboxes, bubbling tanks, smoking flues, hissing valves and clanking pistons. It was hot, grimy, thankless work, and so long as the boat developed her normal dead-water speed of about twelve miles an hour, their efforts went largely unnoticed.

William J. Gamble, who owned an interest in the boat, was also her first clerk. (The arrangement itself was not out of the ordinary, since the clerk, in his dealings with passengers and crew, was almost an assistant captain. But the division of shares in this particular case, one-sixteenth for the captain and one-eighth for the clerk, was certainly a bit unusual.) In his office off the main cabin, Gamble performed all the functions of ticket, freight and business agent. He hired and fired the crewmen, made out the payroll, collected fares and fees and assigned the staterooms. It fell to the lot of the second clerk, William Stratton, to check travelers and cargo aboard at the worst landings. As a consequence, his shoes were frequently covered with a generous layer of Mississippi mud and he was often referred to as the "mud clerk."

Like the animals in Noah's Ark, steamboat officers of every kind came two by two. In the steward's department, as elsewhere, this was true. Henry Cross was the chief, and George Slater the assistant. They supervised housekeeping services, saw to the personal comfort of the passengers and presided over the kitchen, with its big wood cookstove.

Also there were two barkeepers. Not regular officers of the boat, they were independent businessmen, and prosperous ones at that. Thomas McGinty and James O'Hara owned the bar outright, and sometimes cleared as much as a thousand dollars on a twelve-day round trip.

Even the fastest packets would stop almost anywhere there was a dollar's worth of business to be had, and the *Sultana* was no exception. Her gangplank hovered above the bow in waiting for the cities, and foot-planks lay ready for instant use at the smaller landings. Since every village, hamlet and plantation was a way point, the boat carried a sizable compliment of Negro roustabouts to wrestle freight. These, added to the deck hands, stokers, watchmen, cooks, waiters and chambermaids, gave the *Sultana* a crew of seventy-two in addition to the eleven officers, plus the two barkeeps—a total of eighty-five in the boat's company. At nightfall on Tuesday the eighteenth of April, 1865, as the *Sultana* passed the swamps and canebrakes of Louisiana, most of them had just eight more days to live.

George Clayton guided the downward-bound steamer, taking her past the mouth of the Red River, last of the tributaries, and nosing her in and out of Baton Rouge, last of the hill cities. Thus he ended his third and final watch of the day, for the pilots worked on a schedule of four hours on duty and four hours off, always following the clock with meticulous precision.

By the time Ingram took the wheel at eight o'clock, the puffing packet was clattering easily along through the "pilot's paradise." All of the islands—seven hundred and fifty of them—were behind now, and ahead the river moved majestically toward New Orleans in a single deep channel, with no wrecks or snags to block its course.

Loungers on deck watched the great sugar plantations slip past in the moonlight. Each bank presented a mile-after-mile panorama of looming, pillared manor houses, with sloping lawns reaching down to the water's edge in front and clumps of Negro cabins behind. Four years earlier—or even three or two—the buildings would have stood out in sharp contrast to the blackness of the night. But now their white paint was fading, and their forms were only lighter shadows dimly silhouetted against the darker background of

23

forest. Occasional lighted windows winked like lonely fireflies, in this region that had once blazed with the glow of countless candles.

At daybreak, on Wednesday the nineteenth, the *Sultana's* deep-throated whistle called children from their breakfasts and brought them clamoring onto the embankments that guarded the approaches to New Orleans. "Steamboat's a-commin'!" Thin, shrill voices echoed against the sun-drenched pilothouse. "It's the *Sultana* from St. Louie!" Small hands waved a greeting as the graceful steamer skimmed along between the levee rims, riding ten feet above street level, towering high above the rooftops.

An hour or so later, at about the same time that Rowberry was putting his mooring lines onto the wharf and cursing his gangplank over the side, a funeral service was beginning in the East Room of the Executive Mansion. On the mahogany coffin was a shield with a silver plate, bearing the inscription: *Abraham Lincoln—Sixteenth President of the United States—Born Feb. 12, 1809—Died April 15, 1865.* Forty thousand mourners marched with the body, and sixty thousand spectators saw the procession pass out of the Executive Mansion, through a mile of sorrowing streets and into the Capitol, where the coffin was placed on a massive catafalque under the imposing dome.

While Washington wept, New Orleans was left to wonder. As soon as the *Sultana* arrived, word of the assassination quickly spread and was soon being discussed at coffee counters and dinner tables throughout the city. Newspaper editors, however, were forbidden by Secretary of War Stanton even to mention the subject, and with remarkable restraint they obeyed the order for another forty-eight hours. In the meantime, although many of those who heard the story accepted it as fact, many others laughed at the "ridiculous rumor" and called it an April hoax.

Mason had secured a convenient berth for his boat, at the foot of Gravier Street—the same spot which had been bloodied sixteen years earlier by the ill-fated *Louisiana*. After seeing his departing passengers ashore with handshakes and bows, the captain plunged into the busy routine of the "turn around." There were boxes and barrels to be discharged into the drays of their consignees, upward-bound freight shipments to be solicited and loaded, stores to be purchased, coal bins to be replenished and empty staterooms to be filled with new passengers. Acting as expediter, Mason kept late hours on Wednesday night and then rose early on Thursday to make sure that each of the myriad details was attended to with dispatch. Every minute at the landing was money lost, and Mason optimistically hoped to get back into the stream at five o'clock on Thursday afternoon.

Local newspapers listed only two steamers scheduled to leave for St. Louis on this Thursday, April 20. Prospective passengers had a choice between Captain Cass Mason's *Sultana* and Captain Ben Taber's *Olive Branch*. Both packets were almost new, handsomely equipped and well officered. Which boat to take? It was one of those pleasant little problems of traveling, and it was solved in the usual ways—a husband left it to his wife, or a wife left it to her husband, or perhaps a coin was tossed. Casually and nonchalantly the unsuspecting made their selection between life and death.

Then, at the last minute, in spite of Mason's best efforts, there was a delay in the loading of freight, and the *Sultana's* departure had to be postponed until the next day.

≋ II ≋

Against
the Flood

≋

Standing at the foot of the gangplank on Friday morning and welcoming the last of his passengers aboard, Captain Cass Mason weighed his misfortunes against his blessings. The balance, he decided, was in his favor. True, he had found it impossible to leave at the scheduled time on Thursday afternoon and had paced the hurricane deck while Ben Taber's boat captured every eye with her solo farewell. But since the *Sultana* had lost several hours at Cairo, this tardiness in clearing New Orleans was not really unexpected. Riverboats had never been noted for their promptness, had never moved with monotonous punctuality and, in these turbulent times especially, late departures were more the rule than the exception.

It was also true that the *Sultana* had little freight

to haul back north—only one hundred hogs, sixty mules and horses and one hundred hogsheads of sugar. But this, too, was only to be expected. Funneling toward the Gulf's gateway to the world came all the treasures of mid-America—cotton, of course; corn, oats, flour, hay, potatoes, iron, tobacco, bacon, pickles, apples, whiskey, lumber, wool, copper, cloth, glassware and countless other agricultural commodities, raw materials and manufactured products. The *Sultana* had carried such cargoes and this southbound traffic provided Mason and his fellow captains with more than two-thirds of their total tonnage; every captain expected to carry less cargo upriver than down.

Still the *Sultana's* agents had been able to find something for her to take back, even though it was principally livestock, that most disagreeable of freight. And in the matter of passengers, business was brisk. All in all, Mason told himself, it promised to be a tolerable trip.

Having reached this conclusion, the captain tilted the ends of his mustache and, with a cheerful smile, greeted his guests and ushered them aboard. He touched a solicitous hand to the elbow of a plump, handsome young woman with long brown hair and blue eyes—Mrs. Sally B. Woolfolk of Hickman, Kentucky. Fingering the bill of his cap he bade a pleasant good morning to a Mrs. Hoge and to a pair of ladies accompanied by a seven-year-old girl.

Up the curving stairway from main to boiler deck climbed the sizable Spikes family—Samuel B. Spikes and his wife, Elethia, of Assumption Parish, Louisiana; followed by Elizabeth Spikes and two other adult daughters; eighteen-year-old DeWitt Clinton Spikes and another son; and by a niece, Adeline Spikes.

Into the clerk's cubbyhole stepped Seth W. Hardin, Jr., buying tickets for two. Earlier in the war he had served as adjutant of the 3rd Illinois Infantry. Now he was a partner, with his brother Isaac N. Hardin and William H. W. Cushman, in the Chicago banking firm of Cushman, Hardin and Company. With his bride of a few weeks, he was returning home from an extended wedding tour.

Families old and new, women both pretty and plain, and children of all sizes joined the wharf-to-gangplank parade. But most of the passengers were men traveling alone on business, like the nattily dressed J. D. Fontaine of Dallas City, Illinois, and William Long of Leavenworth, Kansas.

Long was carrying a considerable sum of money and prudently decided to deposit it in the office. He handed chief clerk Gamble two packages, one containing five hundred dollars in currency and the other two hundred. Making sure that the passenger's name and address were written on each package, Gamble placed them in the safe.

A much larger amount of cash, however, remained in the possession of its owners. Mr. and Mrs. Spikes, who were moving to the North, had their life's savings with them. Keeping this fact discreetly to themselves, they secreted seventeen thousand dollars in gold somewhere in their stateroom.

At the opposite end of the financial scale were the deck passengers—men who were forced by necessity to travel as cheaply as possible. One of these was

Daniel McLeod, crippled veteran of an Illinois infantry regiment. At the Battle of Shiloh, in the spring of '62, his right knee had been shattered by a musket ball. After spending the better part of three years in hospitals and on limited duty, he had at last been discharged. His useless leg had been examined by the pension surgeon at Springfield, Illinois, and he was now being compensated at the rate of eight dollars a month, the maximum amount paid for total disability.

McLeod, Long, the Spikes family and a majority of the others were on their way to St. Louis. Fontaine, the honeymooning Hardins, and several more had booked passage to Cairo. And the attractive Mrs. Woolfolk was one of the dozen or so who planned to leave the boat at some smaller river town.

Altogether, by the time the *Sultana* at last backed away from the Gravier Street wharf at ten o'clock, some seventy-five men, women and children had been settled aboard. Mason noted with approval that most of the boat's seventy-six cabin berths were filled, although, as usual, the combined total of deck passengers and crewmen remained well below the permissible three hundred.

As they leaned against the rails and waved their last good-bys, on this Friday morning, the *Sultana's* passengers did not know that at this very moment, many miles away in Washington, another journeyer was beginning an odyssey which would overshadow their own. Abraham Lincoln's funeral train was beginning a seventeen-hundred-mile course that would wind through Baltimore, Harrisburg, Philadelphia, New York, Albany, Utica, Syracuse, Buffalo, Cleveland,

Columbus, Indianapolis, Chicago and finally to the tomb at Springfield, Illinois. The new President, Andrew Johnson, Grant, Stanton and thousands of the lesser-known gathered at the depot. Silently they watched the mahogany coffin loaded aboard a seven-car train and saw it pulled away by a locomotive named *Union*. Millions upon millions of people would mark its passings and pausings with tears and tributes.

Yet before the burial twelve days hence, Captain Cass Mason's steamboat would also become a coffin. And while death's lone victim borne by the *Union* would be long remembered, its hundreds of victims aboard the *Sultana* would be quickly forgotten. In the excitement of mourning the one, the many would be ignored.

Since the *Sultana's* arrival at New Orleans, the annual spring flood had come slipping downstream, and the morning edition of the New Orleans *Times* reported: "The rapid rise in the river for the past two days has brought the great Father of Waters upon many portions of the upper landing. We noticed last evening that the steamer *Olive Branch*, in order to get her passengers on board, had to place her staging on the wharf. Many of the planks on the wharf are loosened by the water, and is very dangerous to levee pedestrians. Another foot of a rise will inundate the entire landing."

Once more the mighty river had wakened from its winter sleep and was rampaging south. Again, as almost every year at about this time, thawing snows were combining with seasonal rains to swell a hundred ordinarily slow and shallow tributaries. These distended branches, coursing across the nation's heartland, rushing from east and west, were pushing their burdens into the mainstream and turning it into a raging giant.

Despite his size and strength, however, the Old Man had a weakness which Clayton, Ingram and all other pilots had long since learned to exploit. Upward-bound helmsmen knew better than to meet their adversary face to face. Instead they clung to the banks and moved through the slack inshore water, thus avoiding the full force of the midstream current by slipping around the monster's blind side.

It was exactly this course which the *Sultana* pursued as she shouted her defiance at the Old Man and churned out of the crescent-shaped basin. With her whistle howling mournfully, the big packet skimmed along the harbor's edge, almost scraping the sterns of other vessels at the wharf, heading for the hill cities and home.

For two days and nights the boat plowed north without incident, calling at Baton Rouge and Natchez and at dozens of way points in between. But her progress, because of the contrary flood current, was uncommonly slow. Three hours after sunup on Sunday morning, April 23, she was still more than seventy-five river-miles south of Vicksburg.

Cass Mason had just finished breakfast when his engineer, Nathan Wintrenger, shuffled into the cabin and told him that one of the boilers had sprung a leak. It was not the first time that the captain's equanimity had been disturbed by this dour-faced man.

For months now the boilers had been a source of frequent, almost constant, annoyance. On the previous trip, the boat had been forced to stop at Natchez for their repair. And on the trip before that, at Vicksburg.

Wintrenger indirectly blamed the chronic difficulty on Randolph Elder of Scotland, although he probably did not know the inventor's name. In 1862, Elder had developed the marine fire-tube boiler, and twelve months later, the *Sultana* had become one of the first packets to be equipped with this new contrivance. The old-style boiler was nothing more than a big kettle with a steam receptacle on top and a firebox underneath. But in the Elder boiler, flames and hot gasses from the firebox were passed up through the water tank by dozens of close-packed tubes, thereby increasing the transfer of heat and improving efficiency. In the *Sultana's* case, each boiler contained twenty-four five-inch tubes.

This scheme, Wintrenger was willing to admit, was fine for the Upper River, where the water was comparatively clean and clear. But south of Cairo, he complained, the tiny spaces between the tubes quickly became clogged with sediment. This, of course, prevented the free circulation of water, which led to iron-eating rust and corrosion. Sometimes the mud also built worrisome and dangerous little dry pockets —worrisome because here the metal often became red-hot and burned through; dangerous because, if the water ever broke into one of these molten cavities, an explosion could result.

Apparently the *Sultana's* latest trouble gave added justification to Wintrenger's belief that tubular boilers were unsuited for use on the Lower River. Before the boat left St. Louis, on April 12, the tubes and tanks had been cleaned as thoroughly as possible. John Maguire and John Shaffer, the local marine inspectors, had examined them, had pronounced them in good condition and had issued the usual certificates of safety. Yet now, only eleven days later, a trickle of water was oozing between two warped plates and dribbling down the side of the middle-larboard boiler.

Although engineers were ordinarily expected to make repairs on the run, Wintrenger told Mason that this was another of the times it could not be done. It was impossible to work on the damaged plates while the metal was hot, he declared, and it was dangerous to continue upstream until the rupture was sealed. Reluctantly but firmly he refused to go any farther until the fires were pulled, the boiler cooled and a patch riveted into place.

Resigned to his engineer's judgment, Captain Mason agreed to stop at Vicksburg long enough for the job to be accomplished. He was well aware that a lengthy layover could easily upset the delicate balance between profit and loss. But he gave no hint of concern as he informed the passengers that there would be a slight delay at Vicksburg, due to some small difficulty in the engine room.

When the *Sultana* swung into the wharf at four o'clock on Sunday afternoon, both Wintrenger and Clemens were standing by the boilers ready for action. Immediately, with loudly shouted orders, they pushed their smutty, glistening stokers to the task at hand. Bucket after bucket of muddy river water was sloshed into the fireboxes, raising white sizzling clouds of pungent steam. Then with long-handled rakes the smoldering coals were drawn from the grates, gathered in the buckets and gingerly dumped overboard.

Without waiting for the gangplank, one of the firemen sprang onto the wharf and went racing toward town. His path lay along a zigzagging brick roadway which slanted up the cliff face like a jagged red scar. In his head he carried a message for Klein's Foundry, requesting the services of a boiler mechanic and riveting hammer. He repeated the message to himself with every step as he scurried up the precipitous slope, his toes scuffling and clutching at the bricks, which were set at an angle to provide a sure footing.

Traveling the same sharp incline in the opposite direction was another man in a hurry, the *Sultana's* local business agent, side-stepping downhill like a crab. When he arrived on the landing, just as the big stage was lowered across the steamer's bow, he climbed directly to the hurricane deck and greeted Mason with exciting news.

Near Vicksburg, reported the agent, was a neutral exchange camp filled with paroled Federal prisoners— men recently released from the Confederate stockades. On Friday the departmental army commander had ordered these men shipped north in groups of about one thousand. The *Henry Ames* had taken away the first thirteen hundred and Ben Taber had just cleared port with another seven hundred aboard the *Olive Branch*. But there were still hundreds at the camp awaiting transportation, and it seemed likely that the *Sultana* would be selected to carry a load to Cairo.

Under ordinary circumstances, of course, such mass shipments would have been dealt with by the district steamboat inspector as a gross violation of authorized carrying capacities. But during the war, the regulations governing steamboat passenger limits, like many other laws, had frequently been ignored by the military. In the name of necessity or expediency, large numbers of soldiers had often been crowded onto inadequate vessels, and civil officials had found themselves powerless to interfere.

Any qualms which Mason may have felt at the thought of seeing as many as a thousand men marched onto the *Sultana* were quickly calmed by a consideration of the profit involved. For the captain knew what such a load could mean in terms of dollars. A standard price for the movement of Union troops had been established two years earlier. At that time, after the fall of Vicksburg, Grant had allowed many of his veterans to return home on furlough. Learning that unscrupulous steamboat captains were charging the men exorbitant rates, he had put an end to such abuses once and for all. By his order the cost of passage between any two points on the river had been set at five dollars for enlisted men and ten dollars for officers. In addition to her regular income, the *Sultana* could realize something in the neighborhood of five thousand dollars for less than a four-day haul. Here was an unexpected nugget of luck for Mason, which would far outweigh the late departures, lack of freight, leaky boilers and any number of similar misfortunes. His bearded face beamed at the prospect.

The captain's pleasure was as nothing compared

to the unbounded joy of the men who would soon become his passengers. For they were the survivors of Andersonville and Cahaba, living skeletons ransomed from hell and now poised almost miraculously on the brink of home-coming.

≈III≈

Rendezvous at Vicksburg

Behind Vicksburg, beyond the clump of chimneys and church spires, the Chickasaw Bluffs curved away in a series of uneven undulations, reaching almost a dozen miles to the east. Here the land dipped sharply down and met the western bank of the Big Black River, a sluggish stream which meandered along in meaningless crooks and turns until it ran into the Mississippi at Grand Gulf, some twenty-five miles below.

During the Vicksburg campaign, in the summer of '63, Grant's engineers had built a pontoon bridge across the Big Black River and over this floating pathway of barrels and planks, through the city's back door, the Northern commander had led his troops to victory, driving the Southern defenders into their

fortress and starving them into submission. Originally
the bridge had nestled in a thick forest of blackjacks
and pines. But the contending armies had cut the
timber to make room for their encampments, leaving
a broad belt of bare ground for two or three miles on
either side of the stream.

In the spring of '65 this clearing lay peaceful and
quiet, the scenes and sounds of battle having long
since passed it by. Yet the silent open space with its
wobbly cleavage of water still possessed a certain distinction and importance. Here, the Big Black River
had become a dividing line between the forces of blue
and gray. On one side was the twelve-mile strip, including Vicksburg, held by the Union; the opposite
bank unrolled into the states of Mississippi, Alabama
and Georgia, the last beleaguered stronghold of the
Confederacy.

Up on the western slope, high enough to command
a view of the entire clearing, was a well-kept Federal
outpost—a neat, single file of white canvas shelters
stretched out parallel to the river, garrisoned by two
platoons of infantry. In front of the headquarters tent
stood a tall staff with a United States flag fluttering
from its tip.

Late on the afternoon of March 22, a band of eleven
hundred exhausted marchers arrived at the eastern
edge of the clearing, on the Confederate side. As the
column leaders stumbled out of the forest, they at
once caught sight of the Union camp, lying beyond
the river, about four hundred yards away. For a long
moment there was no sound. Then one man lifted a
frail arm and pointed a fleshless finger.

"Look at the flag!"

Others swarmed out of the woods to stare and shout —a ragged collection of human scarecrows, wasted by sickness and starvation, trembling with the happiness of hope reborn and life regained. Cheer after cheer was raised, and many wept unashamedly. Bony hands clasped together, camp-meeting style, and scurvy-swollen lips sang a discordant chorus of "Rally Round the Flag, Boys!"

The eleven hundred had begun their journey from the Confederate prison stockade at Cahaba, Alabama. For twelve long days and nights they had wound through the lair of the enemy, by riverboat and rail to Jackson, and then thirty miles afoot. Doubt and uncertainty had traveled with them all the way, gnawing at them, whispering to them that the promised exchange was only another Rebel trick.

But now, suddenly, they found themselves within sight of the Federal lines, and Old Glory was waving a welcome. For almost an hour the men indulged in a wild outburst of singing and shouting, releasing all their anxieties in a mighty roar of rejoicing.

Afterward, the soldiers set about gathering firewood and began settling down to their last restless sleep in Rebeldom. Most were up before the sun, in time to watch the river take shape out of the darkness and to see the Stars and Stripes raised on the distant hill. Then the matchless moment arrived. At the near end of the pontoon bridge stood a Confederate officer with the roster of prisoners in his hand. As each man's name was called, he stepped onto the span and walked into the Federal lines. Waiting to receive the repatriates on the Union side was a ramrod-straight lieutenant, who looked with pity and compassion on the parade of shoeless, skeletal men. Some moved toward him slowly, while others almost ran. One paused as he passed, and pointed to a nearby heap of earth. "If that hill were solid gold," he said, "and if you could give it to me to go back to the Rebel horrors for a week, I wouldn't consider it for a moment."

It was well along into the afternoon before the last name was read and the last man, frantic with anxiety, walked over the bridge. When the transfer had finally been completed, the prisoners were loaded onto a string of waiting flatcars and went jolting away toward Vicksburg. An hour later, eight miles down the track, the train crossed a trestle and came to a grinding stop. The trestle was known as Four Mile Bridge, because it was just that distance from Vicksburg, and close beside it was an old, abandoned camp site. Here the men were to bivouac temporarily. During their stay at Camp Fisk, as the place was called, they were to be clothed, fed and sheltered by the Federal government. Technically, however, they were to remain in the custody of the Confederacy until a formal exchange or parole could be arranged.

More than two years had passed since Federal prisoners had been returned to their own lines. Grant himself had broken off the routine trading of captives, in the winter of '63, by presenting Southern agents with a number of difficult demands which he knew would not or could not be met. Later, with characteristic bluntness, he had explained why: "If we commence a system of exchange which liberates all prisoners taken, we will have to fight on until the whole South is exterminated. If we hold those caught they amount to no more than dead men."

Thus the Confederacy had been deprived of manpower it could not afford to lose and it had been burdened with thousands of Union captives at a time when its own ragged troops were starving in the field. As a result, the hastily built Southern stockades, glutted with humanity, had become reeking, lice-infested, scurvy-ridden, maggot-breeding pestholes of suffering and death. With its farms and factories ruined by a shortage of labor, its medical stores and other imports choked off by the naval blockade and its supply lines hopelessly disrupted, the disintegrating Confederacy simply had not had the wherewithal to provide for the swarms of Yankees gathered up by its still unconquered armies. Admitting as much, the Rebel leaders had repeatedly sought an exchange. But Grant, intent on shortening the war, had stood firm. "It is hard on our men in Southern prisons not to exchange them," he had said, "but it is humanity to those left in the ranks to fight our battles." Not until the war was all but over, in this spring of '65, had Grant finally agreed to a man-for-man trade.

"This way to the commissary, men!"

No second invitation was necessary. Through painful neglect, no food had been brought out to the prisoners during their wait at the Big Black River. Since they had marched from Jackson with only an excuse for rations, their latest fast had been extended to three full days. Now, with delight, they piled off the train and flocked to a sizable tent nearby. Widely grinning commissary sergeants kicked open box after box of hardtack and dried beef. Big wooden barrels were rolled out, one after another, and the heads were knocked in, releasing the mouth-watering aroma of pickled cabbage. In a happy, shouting, shoving line the men paraded through the canvas paradise again and again, dipping their eager hands into its inexhaustible treasures, licking their fingers and smacking their lips, gorging themselves and fulfilling a dream.

Not all, however, were able to participate in the feasting. Long months of denial and disease, and then the two-day trek from Jackson, had left many too weak and ill to think of food, especially such rough fare as that available at the commissary tent. Scores were suffering from the cold sweats and griping nausea of dysentery, the bleeding gums and pasty mouths of scurvy, the trembling and faintness of malnutrition, the scales and parasites of slighted hygiene. Their need was for hot baths, clean hospital beds, competent doctors, attentive nurses, proper drugs and a nourishing diet prepared by experienced cooks. Instead they were offered hardtack, dried beef, pickled cabbage and, for the time being at least, nothing else. No medical attention of any sort, no blankets whatever, no article of clothing awaited their arrival. Only a dozen or so tents had been pitched, enough to accommodate a trifling thirty or forty. And as night fell, the remaining hundreds were left to dot the darkness with campfires and lie down to sleep on the bare ground.

Most of the men spent their first full day of freedom

trying to provide themselves with some kind of shelter. Near the camp site was a canebrake swamp, and this marshy thicket was soon full of industrious Yankees. Using borrowed axes, they cut the leafy reeds and made lean-tos and pallets. One group, wandering farther afield, found a deserted barn and made themselves at home in its inviting hayloft.

On the second morning a quartermaster belatedly arrived from Vicksburg with a generous quantity of supplies. But when an anxious crowd appeared at his store-tent and asked for blankets, he found it impossible to oblige them. Through an oversight, he explained, he had been given no stationery, and if he were to issue the blankets without getting proper receipts, he might have to pay for them himself. Although his attitude was courteous and sympathetic, he declared that he certainly could not take the risk of losing four or five thousand dollars of his own money.

Unable to cope with the first rush of returning prisoners, the authorities at Vicksburg soon found themselves caught up in a flood of new arrivals. The Union prisoners came pouring into the neutral camp with the same disconcerting speed which had swamped the Southern stockades. The last group from Cahaba, almost thirteen hundred, reached Four Mile Bridge on March 25, only three days behind the first contingent. And then came the men of Andersonville, arriving in tattered groups of five to eight hundred, at intervals of three or four days. Back in August, at the peak of its horror, more than thirty-three thousand men had been crammed onto Andersonville's twenty-seven acres of barren, burning sand. But by now, through death and transfer, the population of the infamous Georgia compound had been reduced to roughly six thousand, and only about half this number—the Westerners—had been marked for delivery at Vicksburg. The other half, those belonging to Eastern states, were to be shipped to the Atlantic seaboard for transportation to Camp Parole, near Annapolis, Maryland.

By the first week of April, Camp Fisk had grown into a restless community of five thousand. Hunched over steaming canteen cups of Uncle Sam's fragrant morning coffee, squatting in the midday shade of makeshift huts and sprawled by the side of nighttime fires, the gaunt but grinning refugees traded tall true tales and waited impatiently for the next leg of their journey home. Among them could be found Pap Thomas' boys and Billy Sherman's and grizzled troopers who had ridden through the Shenandoah with Phil Sheridan; veterans of Murfreesboro, Chancellorsville and Gettysburg; men captured at Kenesaw Mountain, Yellow Tavern and at dozens of obscure but deadly little crossroads skirmishes; farm boys from mid-America's rich bottom lands, clerks from its cities and mountaineers from its craggy steeps; men named Murphy and Johanssen and Steiner; immigrants who spoke with an accent, first-generation citizens and men whose forebears had wintered at Valley Forge; men who had languished in the bloated Southern prisons for three months, ten months, two years; lean men blackened by weather, tormented by festering sores and bent with aching bowels.

It was still a canebrake camp, the inhabitants being protected only by such shelter as their own ingenuity could devise. But there was no scarcity of hardtack and beef, and, the requisition forms having finally arrived, an abundance of new uniforms and blankets were available. Other necessities and luxuries were provided by the Christian Commission, a charitable organization which worked untiringly for the comfort of Northern soldiers in the Western theater's field camps and hospitals. Like a flock of ministering angels the ladies of this group—Sisters of Charity they were called—descended upon the returning prisoners, offering fresh vegetables, toilet soap and writing materials for letters home.

"Everything was excitement here," wrote a Michigan cavalryman. "News came of the fall of Richmond and the surrender of Lee. Everybody was wild with joy and the thought of a speedy return to our homes. Salutes were fired from all the forts. Our joy, however, was of short duration, for as we got up one morning we found the colors at half mast. It was some time before we knew the cause, and then we learned that President Lincoln had been assassinated."

At first the men heard only that "a Rebel" had fired the fatal shot. An indignant crowd quickly gathered and with angry shouts and threats of revenge surged toward the tent occupied by a Confederate major who was in nominal charge of the camp. One look at the enraged mob was enough to send the major fleeing on horseback down the railroad tracks and across the pontoon bridge, into the sanctuary of his own territory.

For several hours he remained discreetly withdrawn, until the prisoners heard a more detailed report and relaxed into a less dangerous mood.

But even the news of the assassination, sad and sobering though it was, could not long dampen the soaring spirits of the frail men who thronged Camp Fisk. In a near frenzy of happiness they waited in this land of limbo between two rivers—the Big Black now behind and the Mississippi just ahead—buoyantly thankful that they had survived.

By mid-March the signals of spring, riotously twittering mockingbirds and swiftly growing greenery, surrounded Vicksburg. Through the window of his headquarters office, on the second floor of what had formerly been one of the city's finest homes, Major General N. J. T. Dana could hear the songs and see the leaves, and he regarded them thankfully. In this soothing season the two-star warrior found it easy to cross his legs, lean back with a good cigar and enjoy the fact that the long war was drawing to a close.

Abruptly the general's reverie was interrupted by a respectful tapping on the door. Grunting an invitation, he straightened up and swung his elevated foot to the floor. An orderly entered the room, delivered a telegram which had just been received from the War Department and took his leave through blue swirls of tobacco smoke.

From the scribbled paper Dana learned that arrangements had been completed for the exchange of prisoners of war. Union captives arriving at Vicksburg, according to the wire, would belong to the Western states and should be forwarded to Benton Barracks, Illinois, or Camp Chase, Ohio.

The message failed to mention just how many men were involved, or what their physical condition might be, or where they were coming from, or by which route they would arrive or when they could be expected. But this total lack of detail failed to disturb Dana's tranquillity. No wrinkles of worry creased his moon-round face, and no agitated fingers played through his neatly trimmed beard. Most of his forty-three years had been spent in uniform, and he had disciplined himself to accept such vagaries with a minimum of exasperation. As the result of long suffering, he had attained that splendid and unshakable resignation which is the old soldier's outstanding characteristic.

Dana had begun life as an "army brat," the son of a career officer, at Fort Sullivan, Maine. Graduating from West Point at the age of twenty, he had first seen combat in the Mexican War and had been badly wounded in the storming of Telegraph Hill. Lincoln had signed his commission as brigadier general in the fall of '61 with the remark that his full name, Napoleon Jackson Tecumseh Dana, would "certainly frighten the enemy." A year later, while leading a brigade of the II Corps at Antietam, he had been struck down by an artillery shell which disabled him for months. Following his return to active duty and his subsequent promotion to major general, he had served at Philadelphia and in Texas before coming to Vicksburg.

As commander of the Department of Mississippi,

Dana was responsible for both the District of Vicksburg and the District of West Tennessee. Inevitably, in ruling eighty thousand square miles of occupied territory, his days were plagued by administrative problems, some important and some petty. At first glance, he was inclined to regard the latest War Department telegram as one of the minor perplexities.

Upon reflection he decided that Camp Fisk, which had been little used since the siege, would be the most suitable place for receiving and lodging such returning prisoners as might come his way. Assuming that they would arrive in small contingents, and also assuming that each contingent could be shipped north before the next arrived, he estimated that a temporary billet large enough to accommodate a few dozen men at a time would be more than sufficient. Acting on this conclusion, he ordered his quartermaster and commissary departments to pitch the necessary tents and stock the camp with proper supplies of rations.

Hardly a week later the vanguard from Cahaba came shouting and singing up to the Big Black River. Even Dana was momentarily taken aback by the report that a horde of eleven hundred hungry, half-naked troopers were waiting at the pontoon bridge.

Nor was this the only disconcerting news. Dana had understood that the prisoners were to be released on parole. But he quickly learned that this view was not shared by Colonel H. A. M. Henderson, the Confederate exchange agent, who had accompanied the men to the neutral ground. Henderson told Dana that his instructions called for nothing less than an on-the-spot trade. He flatly refused to turn over any Federal prisoners unless and until he received an equivalent number of Rebel captives in return.

Camp Fisk thus became a depot with only one door —an entrance but no exit—and the prisoners began piling up. Dana spent hours arguing with Henderson and with Colonel N. G. Watts, who was escorting the prisoners from Andersonville. But he got nowhere. Both stubbornly insisted that their charges could not be released on parole without authorization from Colonel Robert Ould, the C.S.A. Commissary General of Prisoners. Dana promptly dispatched a message to Ould, but it drew no response. Richmond had fallen into Federal hands and the Rebel officials had fled— no one knew where.

What had first appeared to be a minor perplexity had developed into a major muddle, which was making an ever-increasing demand upon Dana's time and testing his even temper to its limit. At this point, in normal army fashion, the general decided to turn the whole frustrating problem over to a subordinate.

The man he selected was Captain George A. Williams of the 1st U. S. Infantry. As the departmental commissary of musters, he was expected to maintain a detailed record of all personnel assigned to the command. It therefore seemed logical to Dana that he should also count the men at Camp Fisk and, if possible, hasten their departure.

Dana summoned Williams upstairs to his office, gave him the high-sounding title of Assistant Commissioner of Exchange, and sent him forth to negotiate with the Rebel agents. When the colonels-in-gray next returned from Alabama and Georgia, they were confronted by the captain-in-blue. But Williams had no better luck than his superior. Henderson and Watts still said no.

During the second week in April, acting on Dana's orders, Williams boarded a southbound train for Mobile, where he hoped to procure an official copy of the prisoner-exchange agreement. Failing in this, he was later instructed by telegraph to proceed to Western army headquarters at Cairo for consultation with General Grant, who had lately arrived in the Illinois city fresh from his Virginia victory.

Shortly after Williams left Vicksburg, a volunteer stepped up to take his place. Captain Frederic Speed, adjutant general, Department of Mississippi, offered to assume responsibility for Camp Fisk and its problems—a suggestion which Dana readily accepted.

Then on Tuesday, April 18, the day that the *Sultana* cleared Vicksburg on her way downstream, the impasse was unexpectedly broken and the door that led from Fisk to freedom was suddenly open. Dana had received a reply through channels from the hard-to-find Ould, authorizing Henderson and Watts to release their prisoners on parole-of-honor, pending formal exchange. The news reached the exchange camp and went racing down the dusty streets, hopping from group to group like wildfire. Untethered at last, the prisoners were wildly anxious to be on their way.

According to his own official report, Dana's plan for expediting the departure of the soldiers was simple and direct. He ordered Speed "to prepare their rolls as rapidly as possible and send them north as rapidly as the rolls could be prepared, calculating, as near as circumstances would permit, about one thousand at a load for the regular packets as they passed."

In executing this order, Speed was partially dependent upon Colonel R. B. Hatch, chief quartermaster at Vicksburg, and Captain W. F. Kerns, assistant quartermaster in charge of transportation. While the adjutant general worked at Camp Fisk preparing the rosters, Hatch and Kerns were to maintain a lookout for suitable packets. Speed directed that all steamboats capable of carrying troops be reported to him immediately upon arrival at the wharf.

On Wednesday morning, while the *Sultana* was churning toward New Orleans, Speed began counting the parolees at Camp Fisk by state, regiment and company. First to be assembled were the men of Illinois. Slowly the captain and his assistants inched along the excited ranks, matching individuals against the lists which had been provided by Henderson and Watts. It was a tedious and time-consuming task, for the Rebel rolls proved to be inaccurate and incomplete. As each man identified himself, a mark was placed beside his name. Or if the name could not be found, as was often the case, it was added to the proper page. By sundown the dog-eared sheets bore upwards of six hundred checks and additions.

Next day the process was repeated with the men of Iowa and Missouri. Long lines of painfully slim soldiers straggled in broken formation across the unshaded assembly area. Impatient, but in high good humor, they shouted back and forth, visiting and chattering, their busy feet kicking up nostril-burning puffs of yellow dust. Amid the unmilitary confusion moved the adjutant and his aides, straining to catch names while sweat oozed under their soggy, clinging shirts. Before nightfall another seven hundred had been counted, bringing the total tally to thirteen hundred. And as the camp's myriad fires were rekindled, the Vicksburgh telegraph brought word that Captain Crawford's *Henry Ames* had just steamed in from New Orleans.

Speed lost no time next morning. At gray dawn he began loading the parolees into boxcars at Four Mile Bridge. Even so, moving more than a thousand men into Vicksburg by shuttle train, getting them onto the wharf and then putting them aboard the *Ames* turned out to be an all-day job. When it was done, Dana himself came down to the landing to see the heavy-laden packet steam away with her cheering cargo.

Saturday the counting at Camp Fisk continued— the men of Wisconsin this time—another seven hundred bony boys in blue enrolled and ready for transportation. Nor did they have long to wait. Soon after Sunday breakfast they began marching aboard the *Olive Branch*, and by early afternoon they were joyously watching Vicksburg disappear behind the corkscrew bend.

Ben Taber's packet was barely out of sight when an accusation of bribery was made against Captain Kerns, the assistant quartermaster. Red-faced with rage, Speed burst into Dana's office and asked permission to put the captain under arrest. The *Olive Branch* had tied up at midnight, he stormed, but her arrival had not been reported to him until eight o'clock in the morning. Further, he fumed, the boat had not been allowed to leave for hours after the loading was completed. The adjutant was convinced that there was skulduggery afoot, that Kerns had entered into a conspiracy with the local agent of the Atlantic and Mississippi Steamship Company. For a price, he charged, Kerns had agreed to delay the paroled prisoners until they could be shipped on packets belonging to this line, which held a government troop-carrier contract.

There was not a shred of evidence to back up the allegation. It was based upon nothing more than unconfirmed gossip. But for Speed, the rumor was enough to justify a request, almost a demand, for Kerns's arrest. Apparently the adjutant's outburst resulted more from wounded pride than from outraged virtue. Out of an obvious desire for more authority, he had originally volunteered to take charge of the paroled prisoners, despite the work and worry involved. Now he seemed to be infuriated, not by the whisper of dishonesty, but rather by the suspicion that someone was acting in opposition to his orders.

General Dana, on the other hand, was motivated only by the desire to avoid trouble. With soft words he sought to calm his adjutant's wrath. Pointing out that it would be unwise to act on the basis of hearsay, he advised Speed not to arrest Captain Kerns until he was satisfied that the gossip he had heard was well founded.

The advice was good, but it was not enough. A tragedy might have been averted if Dana had made even a brief inquiry of his own to determine whether his master of transportation was actually guilty of accepting a bribe. But a lifetime of military experience had made Dana a firm believer in the ancient army adage, "He who does nothing makes no mistakes." So when he saw trouble approaching, he simply closed his eyes and hoped it would go away.

Speed's hot temper, however, had not been cooled. He was still seething with anger as he returned to Camp Fisk. Shortly after four o'clock on Sunday afternoon, less than two hours after he began the preparation of a new roster, he received a telegram from Kerns announcing that another packet—the *Sultana* —had just swung into the landing.

On Monday, April 24, it at first appeared that none of the paroled prisoners would be shipped aboard Cass Mason's steamer. Early in the day, Speed reported to Dana that she had arrived too soon after the departure of the *Olive Branch*. Rolls were ready for only about three hundred men—a trifling number in the adjutant's opinion—and he thought it better to wait for the next boat.

But minutes after making this report and leaving headquarters, Speed changed his mind. His about-face was the result of an unexpected meeting with Captain Williams, who had just returned from his futile trip to Mobile and Cairo. In a brief conversation the adjutant brought the commissary of musters up to date on the latest developments and listened to his suggestions.

Later it would be argued that Speed had been placed in charge of the paroled prisoners "during the temporary absence of Captain Williams" and that Williams, upon his return, "immediately resumed the duties of his office." Yet the facts indicate otherwise. All three of the men involved—Dana, Speed and Williams— clearly understood that Speed's appointment had been permanent and that he was still making the decisions.

It was Speed who revisited Dana's office and reported that he had decided to ship all of the remaining prisoners on the *Sultana*. When Dana asked how many men would be involved, Speed replied that there would be about thirteen hundred, certainly not more than fourteen hundred. The exact number could not be given, he said, because of discrepancies in the Rebel rolls. Williams had suggested, according to Speed, that the men be counted and checked as they went aboard. And to all of this, Dana unhesitatingly agreed.

Once the plan had been approved, Speed acted immediately to carry it out. Before the sun had climbed halfway up the eastern sky, he was on his way back to Camp Fisk, where his order to "pack up and get ready to go home" was obeyed with lightning swiftness and thunderous approval. The former prisoners had little to pack; they *were* ready!

Perry Summerville, for his part, had been ready for seven long months. Having enlisted in the 2nd Indiana Cavalry at the age of fifteen, Summerville was a three-year veteran, fighting in Georgia before he was able to grow a respectable beard, and in addition to the hairs on his chin, he had also acquired an enviable duty assignment. Twice a day he rode forth on the Company K forage train, helping to strip the countryside of its finest edibles—sugar-cured hams, corn-fed chickens and wild-berry jams—to provision his comrades in Sherman's army. Of course, the foragers keenly felt a responsibility to sample the quality of any particularly tempting horde they happened to find. But the picnic also had its ants, in the form of guerrilla snipers, snarling watchdogs and home-guard patrols. While making the rounds of plantation storehouses near Stilesborough, Georgia, one crisp autumn morning—September 13, 1864—the young Yank and his detail had the misfortune to ride straight into a Rebel ambush.

When the enemy attacked, with muskets cracking, Summerville immediately jumped from the wagon in which he was riding. In his haste, however, he did not jump far enough. At the instant he hit the ground, sprawled flat on his stomach, a rear wheel of the wagon thumped over his right leg, snapping the bone in two. Left behind by his fleeing comrades, the helpless youngster was picked up by the Rebels and boosted onto the back of a mule. Sometime near noon, ten miles to the southwest, he was transferred to a springless wagon. By the time he was hauled into Jacksonville, Alabama, two days later, his neglected broken leg was a puffy, pain-stitched mass of ruptured tissue, dangerously close to gangrene. Delivered to the Jacksonville hospital, Summerville at last received proper medical attention, along with an unexpected measure of sympathy. While he was confined to bed for a few days, the hospital superintendent treated him with fatherly kindness and gave him a fine comb. And when he was ready to leave, hobbling on a pair of crutches, the superintendent's wife handed him a Confederate ten-dollar bill.

Within two weeks, after brief stopovers at the city jails of Talladega and Selma, Summerville arrived at the moldering village of Cahaba. Here, between the merging Alabama and Cahaba rivers, the hard-pressed Rebels had thrown up a twelve-foot plank fence around a dilapidated brick cotton shed. Castle Morgan the pen was called, in honor of the Confederate cavalry raider, Colonel John Hunt Morgan. Once the gate swung closed behind him, Summerville found himself in the company of some twenty-five hundred others—one man for each seventeen square feet of space. As night approached, Summerville looked about uncertainly for a place to lie down. Inside the roof-less building he discovered a half-dozen five-tiered sleeping roosts—rough hardwood shelves already full of prisoners. Following the example of a thousand others, Summerville awkwardly lowered himself with the help of his crutches and stretched out on the frosty earth floor. Having no blankets, he tucked the crutches under his head for a pillow.

On a visit to the prison hospital, Summerville managed to fashion a knife from a piece of hoop iron, and with this useful implement he prepared and ate his meager rations. Each day, like the other inmates, he received a pint of corn chop, a two-finger-size piece of pork and a tablespoonful of cowpeas, along with one small stick of cook-wood. From the older prisoners he learned to split the kindling into tiny splinters to make a quick fire for boiling gruel. But despite this careful management, there was never enough wood to cook the mixture more than half done. After a time, although his leg was still splinted and sore, Summerville burned one of his crutches. Next, he whittled off half the remaining crutch, leaving himself only a cane. Then one night he forgot to hug his cane as he slept, and the next morning it was gone—stolen by another prisoner to be used at breakfast.

While Summerville and the others were preparing to leave Camp Fisk, Williams hurried down to the wharf at Vicksburg to tell Captain Mason that he could soon expect to receive a full load of passengers. As the two men talked, their voices mingled with the ringing sounds of metal striking metal, which drifted out of the packet's engine room. The mechanic from Klein's Foundry, R. G. Taylor, was busily at work on the leaky boiler; two damaged plates, on the larboard side of the middle-larboard tank, were badly bulged out and clearly needed to be replaced. Mason, however, had declared that any such major repairs would have to wait until the boat reached St. Louis. With his engineer's approval, the captain had told Taylor to cut out only that portion of the boiler wall which contained the ruptured seam—a piece twenty-six by eleven inches. This the mechanic had done, and now he was noisily hammering out a patch to cover the hole. His patching material was one-quarter of an inch thick, somewhat thinner and more pliable than the standard $1\frac{7}{48}$-inch boiler plating.

High above the landing, atop the bluff, the superintendent of military railroads, Mr. Butler, was creating an even louder racket as he hitched one of his locomotives to a string of rolling stock. In a short time he had the shuttle train rattling eastward along its narrow-gauge track. When it reached Four Mile Bridge, the men of Ohio were called, and they eagerly swarmed to the siding and into the cars.

Taxed by the weight of six hundred soldiers, but encouraged by their mighty hurrahs, the little engine lurched into motion, slowly gained momentum and tugged its burden back to the Vicksburg station. In charge of the boistrous caravan was Lieutenant W. H. Tillinghast of the 66th U. S. Colored Infantry, a member of the headquarters staff. From the depot he led the men down the brick-paved street to the wharf and sent them streaming up the *Sultana's* gangplank.

One of the first to be checked aboard was Captain A. C. Brown, late commander of Company I, 2nd Ohio Infantry. Along with most of his men, the twenty-six-year-old Brown had been in Rebel hands since the second day of the Battle of Chickamauga on September 20, 1863. On that fatal Sunday of Union disaster, when the Federal line had broken in two and fled back through Rossville Gap into the safety of Chattanooga, a good portion of the 2nd Ohio had been cut off and captured. Captain Brown's tour of Southern prisons had taken him to Belle Isle and the Smith Building at Richmond, to one of Danville's tobacco warehouses and in April of '64 to the great central compound at Andersonville. After a time, because the Rebels feared that experienced leadership might spark an uprising, he and the other officers had been removed from Andersonville's main stockade to a separate half-acre enclosure nearby. But while the crowding here had been less severe, the rations of unsifted corn meal had been no larger. In his nineteen months as a prisoner, the captain's weight had dropped from around one hundred and seventy-five to about one hundred pounds.

Friends at Cincinnati, upon learning of Brown's release, had extended credit in his behalf, and the Southern Express Company had been authorized to offer any assistance he might require. Brown had made only one request of the agent who visited him at Camp Fisk—that he be provided with stateroom accommodations when it came time for shipment to the North. Now, as he climbed the steamer's first stairway, he saw the agent beckoning to him from the boiler deck. Stepping out of line, he walked over and was introduced to Gamble. The clerk courteously informed him that his cabin passage had been paid to Cairo, where the prisoners were to disembark.

With a good deal less ceremony, Brown's comrades were herded up the second stairway and assigned to the open hurricane deck. Having endured the deadly exposure and packing of Rebel stockades, the men raised no complaint at the prospect of spending a few days on the crowded promenade of a homeward-bound packet. Without a murmur they began spreading their blankets and settling down, cheerfully making the best of their cramped quarters.

No particular effort was made to see that the Ohioans remained on the upper level, however, and a number of them promptly strayed to other parts of the boat. Among the movers were William Boor and William Hulit and their messmates from the 64th Ohio. While boarding the vessel, Boor's attention had been attracted by the sound of hammering on the main deck. So he asked Hulit to keep an eye on his belongings and went down to see what was happening. He poked his head into the engine room, saw the patch being banged into place and decided that the boilers did not look very safe. Making his way back to the hurricane deck he told Hulit and four other companions that they had better find another place to bunk. If they stayed where they were, said Boor, and if the boilers should explode, they would "go higher than a kite." All six thereupon trooped down to the misnamed boiler deck and selected a spot near the stairway.

It was about eleven o'clock on Monday morning when this first load was placed aboard the *Sultana*. An hour later Brown joined the civilian passengers at dinner. As he seated himself at the long table with its rich linen cloth and fragile china, he was struck by the contrast between steamer cabin and stockade. Here, in the finely furnished saloon, he took in the sparkling chandeliers, the well-polished bar, the heavy velvet hangings. And he thought of Andersonville, of its filth and squalor and rotting death. Still suffering from the effects of malnutrition, Brown was careful to eat lightly of the plainest foods on the menu. Then, ignoring the stares of his fellow diners, he gathered up an armful of pastry for his comrades on the hurricane deck. There he found the men going for their rations of hardtack and coffee with a relish.

During the dinner hour, down on the main deck, Klein's mechanic pounded a final rivet into place and packed up his tools. He told the chief engineer that the repair work was neither perfect nor permanent, since he had not been allowed time to remove and replace the damaged plates. Nevertheless he was satisfied with his work and called the patching "a good job."

The *Sultana* was again ready for the river. Wintrenger let Mason know that the fires were being laid and that steam would be raised as quickly as possible. Mason leaned over the rail and shouted to Captain Williams that the boat would leave within two hours. Hearing this news, the commissary of musters spun on his heel and strode angrily off the wharf, up the hill and into departmental headquarters.

Again the walls of the general's office echoed the ugly charge of bribery. Williams was flushed and breathless and his words came in a tumbling torrent of indignation. He reported that the *Sultana* would be gone in an hour or two, and that most of the prisoners were still out at the parole camp. He had been informed, said Williams, that the Atlantic and Mississippi line had offered an under-the-table dollar for every man delivered to its boats. And Speed, he accused, was deliberately practicing delay, intending to hold as many men as possible at Camp Fisk until a boat of that line arrived.

Once more, with the situation demanding firm action, Dana made no attempt to stop such perilous gossip. On the contrary, he did a little talebearing of his own! He replied that Speed himself had made similar charges against Kerns and soothingly suggested that perhaps the commissary of musters "had the rumor wrong." Instead of trying to allay Williams' suspicion, the general merely pointed it in a different direction. He then dispatched a telegram to the parole camp advising Speed that the *Sultana* would soon depart and asking if he intended to put any more men aboard.

, Now both Speed and Williams were convinced that Kerns had agreed to accept tainted money from an agent of the Atlantic and Mississippi Steamship Company. Together they now shared a firm belief that the assistant quartermaster was scheming to induce the shipment of the paroled prisoners on boats belonging to this line and no other. Separately and privately, with a fierceness which blotted out reason, each grimly resolved to load every single man at Camp Fisk aboard the *Sultana*.

Driven by his determination to thwart the suspected fraud and spurred by Dana's telegram, Speed moved on the double. He soon had the boxcars reloaded and rolling with the men of Indiana, but the shuttle train, he decided, could not possibly move all of the paroled prisoners by sundown. In his eagerness to clear the camp before the *Sultana's* departure, he began organizing small marching parties and sending them into Vicksburg on foot.

At the end of the line, Williams was loading the boat systematically, top to bottom and stern to bow. He had assigned the Buckeyes to the hurricane deck, filling the promenade from yawl to stairway. And when the second trainload arrived, he billeted Perry Summerville and his fellow Hoosiers on the boiler deck, where they completely surrounded the cabin.

Since these first two contingents had been grouped by state, regiment and company, Williams had been able to find most of the names on the Rebel rolls and check them off as the men stepped onto the gangplank. But as the afternoon wore on, things grew more confusing. Speed's marching parties began straggling from Fisk to Vicksburg in scattered groups, meeting other groups coming from the train, mingling together on the wharf and becoming hopelessly mixed. Williams needed time to search and scribble, and there was none to spare. Flipping frantically through the unreliable roster, he found it impossible to keep up with the names, and finally he lost track of the number.

One after another, dozen upon dozen, score behind score, the men of Kentucky, Michigan, Tennessee and Virginia trooped onto the landing and spilled over the steamboat's gunwale. Limping and laughing, shuffling and shouting, they passed in a blurring procession. There was a disturbing sameness about them, and a sadness, too, even as they smiled. Nearly all were young—an average twenty or twenty-one years —but they walked with the uncertain gait of age. Most had been stripped of flesh by starvation and their faces wore the haunted look of men misused.

Thick and fast came the men of Michigan, more numerous than the rest, chanting name, rank and unit as they swung aboard . . .

"Stevens, Joseph, Sergeant, Company B, 1st Michigan Sharpshooters!"

In the spring of '64, aching from three years of combat, the armies of blue and gray roused themselves from a winter of inactivity for the final struggle. On the sunlit fourth of May, Grant led his Army of the Potomac down across Virginia's swift-flowing Rapidan River and then set out on the long march that would bring him face to face with Lee at Appomattox Court House. Before that fateful meeting, however, much bloody fighting would have to be done by the men in the ranks.

For Sergeant Joseph Stevens, a twenty-two-year-old veteran with a touch of Yorkshire in his speech, the prospect of a hard campaign held no terror. Orphaned while still in knee pants, soon after his family emigrated from England to America, Stevens had matured early, working at any available job to support his older sister and baby brother. Then, before the echoes of Fort Sumter died away, he had enlisted in the 4th Michigan Infantry and had been toughened in the kiln of war. After fighting at Bull Run, Yorktown and New Bridge, he had been captured during the Seven Days' Battles near Richmond. Confined at Libby Prison, exchanged because of sickness and discharged from the 4th, he had immediately re-enlisted in the Sharpshooters. With this elite regiment he had served against Morgan's Raiders in Ohio and more recently had stood six months of guard duty at Camp Douglas Federal Prison, Chicago.

Yet with all his seasoning, Stevens soon discovered that following the pugnacious Grant involved peril of a special sort. No sooner had the army crossed the Rapidan than it collided head-on with Lee's forces in a tangle of twisted trees aptly called the Wilderness. Almost at once there was a second grinding clash, at Spotsylvania, then a third at Cold Harbor.

On the evening of June 16, 1864, the fast-moving Federals, bone-weary but winning, pushed on to the outskirts of Petersburg. And the next night Sergeant Joe Stevens again found himself on the wrong side of a gun sight. Stevens had just caught a rooster, intending to have a feast for supper, when the Sharpshooters were ordered to move up. Quickly tying the unplucked bird to his belt, the veteran squad leader snatched up his rifle and led his men forward. But this time he charged too far, too fast. He was captured, and the rooster was eaten by the Rebels.

After being searched at the provost marshal's office in Petersburg, Stevens was herded with fifty other prisoners into a creaking boxcar. Eight days later, stiff-legged and blinking, he tumbled out beside a weathered shanty which bore the legend, ANDERSON STATION. Down a mile of sun-baked road and through the dreaded double gates he was marched, to be swallowed up in Andersonville's midsummer nightmare.

Encircled by a breeze-robbing palisade of close-set pine timbers, the milling throng of prisoners stripped the enclosure bare in a clawing search for cook-wood and building materials. Those who had managed to keep their blankets constructed rickety shebangs, while the rest burrowed into the ground like moles to escape the blazing sun. An insufficient creek, the only source of drinking water, became a reeking quagmire of human excrement, spreading cholera and typhoid fever. Provisions of all kinds dwindled to the vanishing point. "The food they gave us was corn cobs, all ground up and made into mush," wrote Stevens, "and there wasn't near enough of that to keep the boys alive any length of time." Each month another battalion of the young and virile were transformed into feeble wretches and each day another hundred died.

"Goodrich, W. N., Private, Company E, 18th Michigan!"

In the summer of '62, when war seemed spangled with splendor and filled with high adventure, nineteen-year-old W. N. Goodrich answered the call to duty. Like most of his chums in rural Lenawee County, Michigan, he one day saddled up his horse and rode over to the recruiting office at the county seat. Upon signing his name and taking his oath—the ceremony was surprisingly sudden—he became a soldier of the United States. With the exaggerated air of self-assurance which suggests a lump in the throat, he kissed his sweetheart good-by, told his parents not to worry, and marched off to win fame and glory on the field of battle.

But somehow it didn't work out that way.

After a short stay in camp at Hillsdale, Goodrich was sent to what he supposed was the front, but was in fact Kentucky. For a long year the 18th Michigan tramped back and forth across the Blue Grass State, serving no useful purpose so far as Goodrich could see. When spring came, the regiment boarded a troop train and moved south to Nashville. A second year passed, with the men spending most of their time killing lice—the "graybacks" and "bodyguards" of soldier slang. Another spring brought another move, this time to Decatur, Alabama. Arriving at night, the 18th pitched its tents on what appeared to Goodrich and his friends to be the garbage dump of the city. Goodrich was, however, fully accustomed to strange orders from his officers.

Finally, as the hot summer of '64 drew to a close, Goodrich found need for his loaded rifle. On a raid against Sherman's supply lines, Nathan Bedford Forrest and forty-five hundred Rebel troopers approached the town of Athens, fifteen miles north of Decatur, intent upon capturing the Federal garrison at that point. To seal off the town and prevent reinforcements from interfering with his plans, the Confederacy's Wizard of the Saddle dispatched his youngest brother, Jesse, to destroy the railroad and cut the telegraph wires between Athens and Decatur.

Late on the afternoon of September 23, a Union cavalry patrol rode into Decatur with the report that a band of Johnnies were tearing up the tracks north of the city. Unaware that the Rebels were raiding in force, the brigade commander at Decatur ordered out a detail of four hundred men, including Goodrich. Boarding a train of flatcars in the night, the nervous Yanks crossed the Tennessee River and waited until sunrise. At first light, they continued north on the cars until they came to a break in the tracks, then formed into column and proceeded cautiously on foot. They had marched only a short distance when they were suddenly fired upon by the enemy.

General Forrest by this time had driven the Athens garrison into its fort and was demanding surrender. After a delay of two hours, the Federal commandant, realizing that he was hopelessly outnumbered, decided to yield. At the moment of capitulation Goodrich and his companions were less than a mile away, gallantly trying to cut a path through Jesse Forrest's regiment. But when the gates of the fort swung open and the boys in blue marched out under a white flag, the detail from Decatur had no choice but to join them in surrender. Stripped of their weapons and equipment, Goodrich and the more than two thousand other captives were promptly moved out to the southeast, on the road to Castle Morgan.

"Robinson, George F., Private, Company C, 2nd Michigan Cavalry!"

As 1864 neared its end, the sands were running low for the Confederacy. Lee was at bay before Richmond, and Grant was near enough to hear the city's church bells. Atlanta had been burned, and Sherman was marching to the sea, cutting a wide swath of destruction and fulfilling his promise to "make Georgia howl." In a last desperate attempt to turn the tide of Union victory, one-legged John B. Hood set out from Alabama with forty thousand ragged but determined Rebels, marching north. By attacking Nashville, which had been in Federal hands for almost three years, Hood hoped to draw Sherman out of the Southern heartland and once more put the Union forces on the defensive.

Among the first prisoners taken by Hood's advancing legion was nineteen-year-old George Robinson of the 2nd Michigan Cavalry. Captured at Shoal Creek, Alabama, on November 5, he was walked and waded back across the Tennessee River to Tuscumbia, where he escaped during the night. Before morning he was recaptured, in time to be loaded aboard a prison train —a mixed string of boxcars and heavily guarded passenger coaches—bound, via Corinth, Mississippi, for the Meridian stockade. But capturing George Robinson was one thing, and keeping him in custody was another problem altogether.

At Meridian, working furtively with flimsy canteen halves and rusty cans, Robinson and six companions soon tunneled under the timbers and wormed their way out. After three days and sixty miles of running, the fugitive Yanks were finally caught, as Robinson reported, "by an old woman and fifteen dogs." Along with the others, Robinson was brought back to Meridian covered with clay and clothed only in shirt, drawers and one shoe.

A month later, while being transferred to Castle Morgan, Robinson and his friend John Corliss jumped out of the car window. Badly skinned and bruised by their leap from the train, the fleet-footed pair stayed in front of the tracking hounds for five days and nights, stumbling through swamps in the cold of December, with nothing to eat but raw corn. Again recaptured, they were once more returned to Meridian, and on the second try the Rebels managed to keep them on the transfer train until it reached Cahaba.

Still not ready to give up, Robinson and Corliss succeeded in escaping from Castle Morgan within a matter of weeks by cutting through the plank fence with a makeshift knife. But on the outskirts of Selma, twelve miles to the north, they were caught and turned over to the local provost marshal for safekeeping. The provost marshal, unacquainted with his prisoners' mettle, locked them in a windowless room on the second floor of his headquarters. Finding a poker in the room, Robinson and Corliss quickly dug a gaping hole in the brick wall, dropped eighteen feet to the ground and ran. Before they could get out of the city, however, they were recaptured and immediately taken back to Cahaba, this time to stay.

"Smith, Truman, Private, Company B, 8th Michigan Cavalry!"

On November 24, 1864, the advance of Hood's army collided with an element of the 8th Michigan Cavalry near Henryville, Tennessee. Following a sharp skirmish the Union commander ordered his men to take cover behind their barricade. In the ensuing scramble one young trooper was left behind. Truman Smith, who had enlisted three months earlier at the age of fifteen, failed to find his horse. Arms pumping, with three Rebel riders thundering at his heels, he dashed into the woods and plunged into a waist-deep marsh. High-stepping along, he succeeded in eluding his pursuers when their mounts became mired in the mud.

For three days and nights, Smith ducked and dodged his way through enemy territory before he finally ran afoul of a Confederate cavalry detachment. He was then marched back to Columbia, Tennessee, and rudely shoved into Fort Misner, an ancient pile of battered stones which had been pressed into service as a temporary prison. When Smith arrived, he found about seven hundred other captives already squatting in the cold, damp interior. With them he shared a jaw-exhausting, stomach-cramping diet of "corn on the cob from once to twice a day."

Three weeks later the bedraggled remnant of Hood's army—bloodied at Franklin by John Schofield and beaten at Nashville by George "Pap" Thomas—turned south in headlong flight. As the dispirited Confederates streamed back through Columbia, Smith and the other prisoners, now two thousand in number, were prodded out of Fort Misner to join the grueling retreat. For ten sixteen-hour days they marched, the hunted Rebels and their Yankee captives, slogging along half frozen through a slashing blizzard of snow and sleet, binding hats and coat sleeves around their feet in lieu of shoes, leaving bloody prints on the icy roads. Upon reaching the rail junction at Cherokee, Alabama, just south of the Tennessee River, the prisoners were locked into stock cars in which fresh horse dung was ankle-deep. A few hundred, including Smith, wound up at Castle Morgan, while the majority were carted at last to Andersonville.

In a steady, unbroken parade, they filed across the *Sultana's* staging—Sergeant Stevens of Andersonville, who had been caught with a rooster on his belt; Private Goodrich of Cahaba, who had finally met the enemy at Athens; Privates Robinson and Corliss, who had been hard to hold; young Private Smith, who had lost his horse near Henryville; and others like them by the hundreds—filling the main deck, shouldering their

73

way onto the already too crowded upper decks and mounting the roof of the texas.

Unused to such weight, the promenade creaked and cracked as if it were about to collapse. A party of deck hands, led by William Rowberry, the chief mate, hastily elbowed their way along the teeming boiler deck, wedging stanchions under the sagging overhead. Despite these emergency props, however, the hurricane deck continued to sway downward to a noticeable degree.

While the loading was in progress, two other northbound packets arrived at the Vicksburg wharf—the *Pauline Carroll* and the *Lady Gay*. Enviously their captains, White and Williamson, watched the troops being marched onto their competitor's boat. Both longed to share in the lucrative business; both were studiously ignored. With a rock-hard resolution Williams continued to squeeze the luckless swarm of parolees aboard Cass Mason's groaning steamer.

Mason by this time was thoroughly alarmed. He had been anxious to make a profit—and still was, for that matter—but he had no desire to see his boat crushed under foot. Throughout the afternoon he had managed to maintain an uneasy silence. But now, as the shadows lengthened with evening's approach, he could keep quiet no longer. Stepping in front of the gangway he held up his hand and halted the marching line. One of the prisoners heard him say that he had enough men on board and could take no more. With an oath Williams replied that he was loading the boat and would put as many men on as he pleased.

A little later Captain Kerns, the assistant quartermaster, made a more persistent, but equally futile, effort to stop the overloading. He first came down to the landing and urged Williams to put half of the prisoners aboard the *Pauline Carroll*. The commissary of musters reacted to this proposal by flying into a near violent rage—the *Pauline Carroll* belonged to the Atlantic and Mississippi Steamship Company. Furious at what he considered a brazen attempt to earn bribery, Williams damned Kerns to hell and warned him to keep out of his way.

Kerns then reported to his superior that the *Sultana*, with two other steamers lying alongside, was being heaped beyond all reason. Colonel Hatch, however, refused to interfere. He had tangled with Speed on more than one previous occasion and had always come off second best. Since the adjutant general was presumed to speak for and with the authority of General Dana himself, the chief quartermaster had learned that it was useless to oppose him.

If Kerns were actually involved in a conspiracy with an agent of the *Pauline Carroll*—and no evidence was ever produced to prove the charge—then he was assuredly among the boldest of rogues. For when he failed to get any help from Hatch he carried his case directly to Brigadier General M. L. Smith, commanding the District of Vicksburg. But Smith also shrugged off the complaint, saying that he had nothing whatever to do with the shipment of paroled prisoners.

And so the loading continued, through the twilight hours and into the night. Long after dark Speed returned to Vicksburg and reported to Dana that Camp Fisk had been cleared, except for a few men from the trans-Mississippi region, who could be sent home by rail and stagecoach. Then the adjutant joined Williams on the wharf to watch the last of the prisoners go aboard.

As the laggards plodded by, the two captains stood side by side near the gangplank. Above them on the steamer hung a flame-filled iron pot which bathed the scene in an unearthly glow, raising ghostly shadows against the bluff.

It had been a long, busy day. Since midmorning Williams had watched a fair sampling of the Union army pass in review. Before his gaze had marched whole platoons of the 40th Indiana, 50th Ohio, 64th Ohio, 100th Ohio and 104th Ohio, all taken by Hood in the Nashville campaign. Among the Athens prisoners he had seen entire companies of the 18th Michigan, 16th Ohio, 102nd Ohio, 9th Indiana Cavalry and 3rd Tennessee Cavalry. Altogether, including a multitude of individuals and squads gathered up from Virginia to Georgia, no less than one hundred and ninety-five regiments were represented on the crumpled pages which the commissary of musters held in his hand.

The total rose to one hundred and ninety-six when Captain W. S. Friesner and his guard detail closed in at the rear. Company K of the 58th Ohio, in full uniform and under arms, was being sent along to escort the parolees to Camp Chase, Ohio.

Speed and Williams did not know exactly how many men they had piled onto the packet, and neither of them crossed the gangplank to see at first hand the result of their handiwork. But as they looked up at the crowded decks, both realized that the boat was out-rageously overloaded.

Even then it was not too late to make amends. The *Carroll* and the *Gay* were still lashed nearby. Yet the two men, talking in hushed monotones under the flickering fire pot, agreed that it would be too difficult to divide the load.

At about one o'clock in the morning, beneath spring's black velvet sky, the *Sultana* cast off her lines and breasted the swirling, swollen Mississippi. Wal-lowing away into the night with her cabin lamps ablaze, she looked like a white three-layer cake, twinkling with birthday candles.

Soon after the departure, the *Sultana's* clerk, Gam-ble, stopped by Captain Brown's stateroom. Seated on chair and bunk, the two men talked of Andersonville and the war. At last Brown interrupted Gamble's questioning to ask how many men were on the vessel. The clerk quickly boasted that if the *Sultana* reached Cairo safely, it would be the greatest trip ever made on the Western waters. There were about twenty-four hundred soldiers, one hundred citizen passengers and a crew of about eighty—in all over twenty-five hun-dred people on board—more than were ever carried on one boat on the Mississippi River.

One fact Gamble failed to mention—the *Sultana's* maximum legal load was three hundred and seventy-six persons, including the crew.

Happily
toward Home

≈≈

Never before had Old Man River seen anything to compare with this spark-tossing packet, and its incredible load of skinny soldiers, which came struggling up against the spring flood of '65. From stem to stern, from rail to rail, from water's edge to the roof of the texas, the *Sultana* was packed. When she steamed out of Vicksburg in the post-midnight darkness, walking the water toward home, there was hardly a foot of unoccupied space on any of her decks.

Inside and out, in every angle and curve, the boat was jammed. A row of double-deck cots had been set up along the center of the main saloon and through the ladies' cabin to provide sleeping accommodations for the officers. Under the brilliant stars the enlisted men stretched out as best they could, shoulder to shoulder, forming a close-laid patchwork of bodies.

All through the night, here and there, the patchwork's lumpy surface was broken by shadowy, restless groups who sat excited and wakeful, puffing their pipes into glowing life, adding an undertone of droning voices to the lullaby of the paddle wheels.

At the first light of dawn, the patchwork rippled and rose and again became more than two thousand men. With a hubbub of conversation, the paroled prisoners happily greeted the morning, shuffling about, shouting to one another, stretching and scratching themselves in the brisk river air.

Henry Cross, the chief steward, shooed the officers out of the cabin, snuffed out the sputtering night lamps and set about replacing the cots with the long dining table. As the aroma of boiling coffee and sizzling bacon drifted over the decks, the men set up a good-natured clamor for breakfast. But while the citizen passengers emerged from their staterooms to enjoy a hot, hearty meal, the soldiers had to content themselves with much simpler fare.

Down on the main deck, Captain Hazellaige of the 40th Indiana, who had been appointed quartermaster for the journey, began distributing the day's rations with the help of an assistant from his regiment, Sergeant C. M. Nisley. Generous quantities of hardtack, salt pork and coffee were doled out to the commissary sergeants of the various regiments, and they in turn made a division among the men. No thought, however, had been given to the matter of preparing the food. A few dozen were able to fry their pork on a small stove located on the fantail, and some succeeded in making coffee with hot water drawn from the boilers. But since there were no camp kettles or mess pans aboard, these makeshift cooking facilities could serve no more than a tiny fraction of the hungry throng. Most simply ate their hardtack and washed it down with sandy river water, procured by lowering quart-sized canteen cups over the side.

No gladder group ever traveled the river. If the rations were light, no matter; if the press of bodies made it difficult to move about, no one seemed to care. For after hope-bereft months or years in Southern stockades, the soldiers were going home—to wives, mothers, fathers, sisters, brothers and sweethearts. Thrilled by the anticipation of these long-awaited reunions and exhilarated by the adventure of being aboard a big Mississippi packet, they were in a holiday mood.

In addition to the never-ending talk of home, the soldiers found a number of other diversions. On a previous trip one of the boatmen had brought a monstrous alligator aboard the *Sultana*. This curiosity—some said it was seven and a half feet long—was kept in a heavy wooden box inside one of the storerooms built into the top of each paddle-wheel housing. Word of the wonder quickly spread and brought a steady parade clambering up to the hurricane deck. Crowding around the storeroom door, the soldiers took turns prodding the huge reptile with sticks, guffawing as it spread its tooth-lined jaws and hissed in anger.

Near midafternoon the troops roared their approval when the Chicago Opera Troupe offered to give a

free concert. Like the soldiers, this company of minstrel men had boarded the *Sultana* at Vicksburg,
taking passage for Memphis to keep an engagement
at the Atheneum Hall. Now, up on the bow, their ban-
jos rang with Foster's familiar melodies and with the
popular soldier songs. Never did blackface performers
sing to greater applause, dance their buck and wing
to louder cheers, tell their end-men jokes to more enthusiastic laughter, or work themselves into such a
frenzied, hand-clapping, tambourine-smashing finale.

Even the sick and injured—and there were scores
of them scattered about the decks—were in good
spirits. Eagerly they leaned on bony elbows to chat
with the ladies of the Christian Commission who
threaded their way along the teeming decks dispens-
ing hymnbooks and quantities of sweet crackers and
other dainties. Twelve of the Sisters of Charity were
accompanying the men north, being escorted by an
elderly Christian Commissioner named Safford, of
North Madison, Indiana. Safford's young son was also
making the trip.

Almost to a man, with the exception of the seriously
ill, the parolees found the journey carefree. But the
Sultana's captain and his officers definitely did not.
Mason was well aware that his boat was dangerously
overloaded, and at unguarded moments his customary
smile gave way to a worried frown. The dour-faced
Wintrenger, making no effort to hide his concern,
nursed his fractious boilers with more than usual
suspicion and watched apprehensively for the next
sign of trouble.

Rowberry, the chief mate, buttressed the sagging

promenade with additional stanchions, tightened the halters which held the skittish herd of horses and mules on the after part of the main deck and fervently wished that he had more bulk freight to use as ballast. Rowberry was thoroughly experienced in the art of balancing a boat, yet even with the hundred hogsheads of sugar carefully stored in the hold, the packet was now so top-heavy with shifting humans that she rolled, slightly but awkwardly, with every turn.

Clayton and Ingram, both skilled helmsmen, were steering against one of the worst spring floods in recent river history and needed all their knowledge and dexterity to keep the unwieldy craft on course. All along its lower reaches the Mississippi was climbing out of its banks, spreading wet fingers far back into the swamps and canebrakes. Miles of interior—miles which had been dry land when the *Sultana* passed downriver—were now covered with up to fifteen feet of swirling, muddy water. For all of its two- or three-mile width, the main channel was a pitching, tumbling torrent, thick-strewn with trees that had been ripped from the soil and now came spinning down with the rise.

Looking for easy water, the *Sultana* hugged the shore line as she pushed upstream. With cypress boughs at times raking her entire length, she crowded up against the forest wall, ducking behind sand bars and slipping through narrow island passages where the water was comparatively still. Often it was necessary to cross the stream, for the most favorable passage lay first on one side and then the other. Upon reaching a crossing point—invisible to the landsman, but marked for the pilots by a familiar stump, stone, tree or the like—the wobbly boat would be sent angling away to the opposite bank, careening with the current and shuddering in noisy protest as the floating logs smacked into her broadside.

At seven o'clock on Wednesday morning, April 26, thirty hours after leaving Vicksburg, the *Sultana* swung into Helena. The prisoners, who were just working out the kinks after spending their first full night aboard, craned their necks to get a look at the town. There was not much to see except a scattering of frame buildings laced together by broad plank sidewalks. Ordinarily this busy town of five thousand— second largest in Arkansas—was an attractive place, but today the Mississippi was washing it with mud and leaving ugly brown pools of water in its streets.

Before landing, the men had been told that the *Sultana* would make only a brief stop, and they had been cautioned not to leave the boat. But if the men could not get off to visit the town, there was nothing to prevent the town from visiting them. Curious and excited, the citizens of Helena abandoned their occupations and came hurrying down to the river front to exchange waves, shouts and stares with the returning prisoners.

Among the onlookers was a photographer—his name has been forgotten—who recognized a remarkable scene when he saw one. Quickly setting up his long-legged tripod on the wharf, he ducked under the black adjusting hood and aimed his heavy lens at the *Sultana*. As soon as the photographer was seen, almost every man aboard scrambled to the rail, determined to get into the picture. With a sickening lurch the off-balance boat listed twenty degrees to larboard. Up on the texas sat Captain J. Walter Elliott, holding to the roof edge with both hands, his feet dangling down into thin air. Expecting the boat to capsize and sink at any moment, he shouted down to the troops, urging them to move away from the rail.

When the war broke out, Elliott, a rangy, rawboned Midwesterner with a brick-red beard, was an Indianapolis lawyer. Answering Lincoln's first call for volunteers promptly, at the age of twenty-eight, he sold his practice for a fair sum and enlisted in the 10th Indiana Infantry. For three years he served with this regiment, rising to the rank of sergeant. Then the Federal government decided, after much discussion and with many misgivings, to enlist Negroes in the army. As a result of this decision, Elliott was given a captaincy, along with command of Company F, 44th Regiment, United States Colored Troops.

Ninety days after taking his eager recruits into the field, the new captain was captured by the Rebels. He remained in custody only a few hours, just long enough to sign a parole giving his promise not to act in opposition to the Confederacy until formally exchanged. Returning to brigade headquarters, he was immediately ordered back on duty, without exchange. Then on the black and bitter night of December 2 in '64, while trying to steal through Hood's lines near Nashville on some obscure errand, he again fell into enemy hands.

Elliott was well aware that if his true identity became known he was certain to be court-martialed and shot as a parole violator, especially since Southerners heartily despised the white officers of Negro troops. So when he was registered at Fort Misner, he assumed the name and command of his cousin, Captain David E. Elliott of Company E, 76th Indiana, whom he knew to be with Sherman on his march to the sea. With his life hanging on the success of this subterfuge, the red-whiskered Yank had spent the winter at Andersonville. And even now, aboard the *Sultana*, he was still clinging to his alias, determined to reveal his real name to no one until he was safely back in the North.

An hour after landing at Helena, the *Sultana* was on her way again, and the second day out of Vicksburg proved to be very much like the first. Once again the ladies of the Christian Commission passed out hymn-books and dainties, and the Chicago Opera Troupe gave another concert. But the alligator was withdrawn from exhibition. Growing tired of the constant poking at their pet, the boatmen removed the reptile from the paddle-wheel house and locked it away in a closet beneath the hurricane-boiler-deck stairway.

As the overburdened boat shoved steadily northward, the air became gradually cooler, and by early afternoon, dark, threatening clouds began gathering and tumbling across the sky. Later, as the sun slipped down toward the larboard rail and at last dropped below the forest on the western side of the stream, the thunderheads became tinted with orange, and a quietness settled over the throbbing packet.

On the lower deck, twenty-year-old Chester Berry of the 20th Michigan leaned back against the engine room partition and relaxed. Behind him lay twenty months of hardship and heartbreak—ten months of soldiering, which had ended with his capture at Cold Harbor, and then ten months of suffering at Andersonville. Ahead the future beckoned, rosy as the sunset.

Berry had spent most of the day thumbing through a hymnbook which had been given to him by one of the Sisters of Charity. In it he had found a song that reminded him of home, and now, as twilight settled around the soldiers, he sang:

> *Sweet hour of prayer, sweet hour of prayer!*
> *That calls me from a world of care,*
> *And bids me, at my Father's throne,*
> *Make all my wants and wishes known.*
>
> *In seasons of distress and grief*
> *My soul has often found relief,*
> *And oft escaped the tempter's snare,*
> *By thy return, sweet hour of prayer.*

Yelps of excitement suddenly broke the vesper spell as the lights of Memphis appeared off the starboard bow. Here, too, the men were sternly instructed to remain aboard, but even while the lines were being made fast, some began climbing the main-deck rails and dropping ten feet onto the rattling plank wharf. Accepting the fact that his charges were not to be denied, Captain Friesner shouted at the retreating backs, warning the men to stay out of trouble and to return promptly.

By seven-thirty, within a half hour of the *Sultana's*

arrival, hundreds of the paroled prisoners had piled
off and were roaming the bluff city's unpaved, dusty
streets. Many found their way to the Soldier's Home,
where they reveled in the almost forgotten pleasures
of a full, hot meal. Others—those who had managed
to beg, borrow or save a bit of money—sought refresh-
ment of a different sort, and the river-front saloons
were soon filled with frail men who had waited a long,
long time between drinks.

Back on the landing, by the dancing light of pitch-
dripping wire baskets of flame, a number of the men
helped unload the sugar. For their labor, and hard
work it was, they were paid seventy-five cents an hour
—high wages for the times. A few of the soldiers, as
soldiers will, added to their pay by "finding a broken
hogshead." Among them was Private Stephen M.
Gaston, the youngest soldier aboard. Gaston, who had
enlisted in the Union army in October of '63 at the age
of thirteen, was just a boy with a sweet tooth, and
along with Private William Block of the 9th Indiana
Cavalry and others, he filled his hat and haversack
with sugar.

Up and down the gangplank passed a number of
cabin passengers, luggage in hand. Going ashore were
the minstrel men of the Chicago Opera Troupe, disem-
barking to keep their engagement at the Atheneum
Hall. Coming aboard was a naval officer, Lieutenant
Harvey Ennis, together with his wife, child and sister-
in-law.

Another of those taking passage for the north was
United States Congressman-elect W. D. Snow of
Arkansas. Although his state was still claimed by the

Confederacy, Arkansas had been out of the war for more than a year and a half, ever since September of '63, when General Frederick Steele had marched into Little Rock with thirteen thousand Federal troops. Early in '64 a loyalist convention, after declaring secession null and void, abolishing slavery, repudiating the Confederate debt and drawing up a new constitution, had supervised the election of state and national officials. Two senators and three representatives, including Snow, had been sent to Washington with Lincoln's approval. But the Congress, after heated debate, had refused to seat them. So the five were back home, hoping to be accepted at a later date. The hope was vain, for reconstruction was destined to become a thing of bitterness and vengeance, and three more years would pass before the readmission of Arkansas.

In the meantime, however, W. D. Snow was a congressman-elect and Gamble treated him with the greatest deference. When he visited the clerk's office to pay his fare and to receive his stateroom assignment, Snow expressed curiosity over the number of persons aboard. Gamble showed him the *Sultana's* books and certificates, which indicated that the boat was carrying 1,966 enlisted men, thirty-six officers and eighty-five crewmen, in addition to the guard company and the citizen passengers.

At about ten-thirty, while the last casks of sugar were being rolled onto the wharf, Mason sent one of his watchmen up to the big brass bell on the hurricane deck. Across the landing rang the insistent clang-clang-clang of impending departure, calling the tardy soldiers back aboard. Dozens were still ashore, re-

88

luctant to leave the congenial atmosphere of nearby
barrooms, and Friesner's guards began rounding them
up.

By eleven o'clock the *Sultana* was settling down to
sleep. Mrs. Hoge; the blue-eyed Mrs. Sally Woolfolk
of Hickman, Kentucky; William Long of Leavenworth,
Kansas; the finely groomed J. D. Fontaine of Dallas
City, Illinois; Captain A. C. Brown of Chickamauga
and Andersonville; the newly wed Hardins of Chicago;
the eight members of the Spikes family; the twelve
Sisters of Charity; the Christian Commissioner, Safford, and his son; Lieutenant Ennis, his wife and
child; Mrs. Ennis' sister; Congressman-elect Snow;
all of the cabin passengers retired to their staterooms.
Inside the saloon, Henry Cross and his waiters set up
the double-deck cots and dimmed the lamps, while out
on the open decks the soldiers once again became a
patchwork of bodies.

Young Gaston and Block carried their sugar-filled
hats and haversacks up to their bunking place on the
texas deck. For several minutes the two boys sat cross-
legged, side by side, talking of home and eating sugar
by the handful. Then, tucking the remainder of their
horde against the pilothouse at their heads, they lay
down to sleep.

Below them the quiet was shattered by a tall Tennessee soldier who had been rudely routed out of a
saloon by Friesner's guards. Weaving drunk and cursing mad, the thin seven-footer was forced across the
gangplank at bayonet point and was hauled up to the
hurricane deck. Twenty-year-old William McFarland
of the 42nd Indiana poked fun at the Tennesseean

and, infuriated, the intoxicated trooper lunged toward his tormentor. But he succeeded only in stepping on a number of innocent men, and was soundly cuffed from all sides.

Down on the next level, William Fies of the 64th Ohio watched Captain Mason come up from below, on his way to the texas. At the head of the first stairway, Mason found the boiler-deck landing a solid, unbroken mass of reclining men. So closely were the bodies packed that it was impossible to step between them. In order to reach the second stairway the captain was forced to crawl around on the rail, while the delighted soldiers hooted and jibed.

Forward of the cabin lay sixteen of the most seriously ill prisoners, under the care of S. F. Sanders of the 137th Illinois, a Cahaba parolee who had been captured near Memphis in August. When the other men of his state had been shipped out of Vicksburg on the *Henry Ames*, Sanders, a hospital steward, had been ordered to remain at the parole camp to help care for the sick. Thus he had been assigned to the *Sultana*, and as far as Memphis he was the only soldier from Illinois aboard.

Now, however, there was another. Epenetus W. McIntosh, a private of the 14th Illinois, had arrived at Memphis on the *Ames* and had gone uptown to see the sights. But he had tarried too long, and the boat had gone without him. McIntosh considered himself in great good luck when the *Sultana* appeared with another load of prisoners and, saying nothing, he climbed aboard with the others and curled up on the boiler deck.

W. C. Porter of the 18th Michigan came back from his tour of the town to find that he could no longer bunk in the empty coalbin which he and several pals had used the night before. The *Sultana* was about to take on fuel and he would have to find new sleeping quarters. After working his way up to the boiler deck, Porter found an unoccupied space between the smoke-stacks, but as he spread his blanket, one of the soldiers nearby said that the spot belonged to another man and Porter resumed his search, stepping carefully among the sleepers. At last he came across another vacancy and was about to claim it, when he was again told that the place was for someone else. Laboriously returning to the stairway, he discovered that there was just room enough to lie down on the landing, with his feet sticking out over the steps.

Porter did not think of it, but other men who had been sleeping in the coalbins decided that the now-empty cargo hold might offer a warm, snug haven. A score or more crawled down the forward ladder into the dark, spacious compartment. Having escaped the overcrowding and dampness of the open decks, they congratulated themselves and pulled the hatch cover into place overhead.

The night before, on an impulse, Captain Elliott had given his cot to a sergeant he had met at the parole camp, and had passed the evening dozing in a chair. Now, as the captain sat reading beneath one of the cabin chandeliers, the grateful sergeant approached and asked if he had secured another cot. Pointing to his hat on a cot nearby, Elliott indicated that he had, but the sergeant said that the bunk was in a hot and dangerous place, just over the boilers. Brushing aside the captain's protests, the sergeant picked up the hat and moved it to another cot, near the after end of the ladies' cabin. A few minutes later, Elliott retired to the cot which the sergeant had reserved, read until his eyelids grew heavy, then fell asleep. Shortly after midnight he was partly aroused as the *Sultana* backed away from the Memphis wharf, but he quickly dropped off to sleep again.

Slanting cross-stream to the Arkansas side of the river, the *Sultana* tied up at a coalyard opposite the mouth of Wolf River. Here, once again, some of the more able-bodied and energetic soldiers fell to with the roustabouts. In less than an hour, one thousand bushels of coal, enough to reach Cairo, were hand-carried aboard in burlap bags.

Like the *Henry Ames* before her, the *Sultana* had left a few men behind when she cast off from the Memphis wharf. One of these, George Downey of the 9th Indiana Cavalry, had telegraphed home for money while at Camp Fisk, and when the boat reached Memphis he had gone ashore to visit friends. Returning to find the *Sultana* gone, he paid a boatman two dollars for rowing him across to the coalyard. As he rejoined his friends Henry Kline and Charles King, on the hurricane deck, Downey excitedly told them how he had managed to get back aboard. Then he lay down, rolled up in his blanket and smiled with relief. "If I hadn't sent home for that money," he said, "I would have been left." A short while later, George Downey fell asleep. He had just an hour to live.

At one o'clock on the morning of Thursday, April 27, with her fuel bins refilled, the *Sultana* left the twinkle of late Memphis lights astern and churned away to meet death, spiraling a trail of smoke through the darkness, leaving frothy footprints on the opaque surface of the water. The night was all black, moon and stars hidden by clouds. An intermittent drizzle was falling, and the threshing of the ponderous paddle wheels reverberated in the humid air, beating a hollow tattoo in the soggy stillness.

George Clayton, the pilot, leaned on the spokes and swung the boat sharply away from the Arkansas bank. At midstream he straightened her up, preparing to steer a slow but safe center passage among a cluster of islands known as the Hen and Chickens. With a long, lonely watch ahead, Clayton was thankful for the company of Rowberry, the first mate. Since Captain Mason had retired, Rowberry was in charge of the boat, and he had climbed up to the pilothouse for a visit.

Down below, Wes Clemens, the assistant engineer, was at his post in front of the straining boilers, beside the rasping engine. Despite the weight aboard, the head-on flood current and the patched boiler, Clemens was maintaining enough steam pressure to push the boat forward at the customary upriver speed of nine or ten miles an hour. All four of the stokeholes stood open, spilling a ruddy glare of light onto the sweating Negroes who scraped up the coal and heaved it into the fireboxes with a liquid grace, carefully spreading each shoveful evenly over the glowing embers.

Aside from the stokers and the three officers on duty —Clayton, Rowberry and Clemens—only a few others were awake. Out on the open decks a scattering of soldiers enjoyed a last pipe or a final word with a comrade. Three or four unfortunate individuals, the victims of dysentery, joined the quickstep parade and took their turns at the after rail. But for the most part the *Sultana* was asleep.

At one-thirty Clayton began feeling his way through the island group. Off to the larboard loomed Island 42, the eighty-acre clump of marsh and mud known as the Hen, and a quarter mile to starboard lay two of the smaller Chickens, Islands 43 and 44, in a north-south line. The pilot took his bearings on the largest island and then gave it a wide berth, noting that its shore line was deep under water. With the river at flood stage, he was taking no chances on losing his heavily loaded boat to a hidden snag or grounding her on a shoal.

At one-forty-five Clayton knew, though he could not see, that he was passing Island 41, a narrow, half-mile strip of sand and trees near the Arkansas side. A quarter hour later, the shape of the river told him that Tangleman's Landing was slipping by on the Tennessee bank. At this point the stream was normally three miles from edge to edge, but tonight it was swollen to at least triple width, inundating the forest that fringed the Tennessee highlands, reaching far back across the Arkansas flats.

And this was the place where death was waiting.

At two o'clock in the morning, suddenly and without warning, the *Sultana's* boilers burst. Hovering rain clouds reflected the eruption's crimson glow, and its thunderous roar echoed off the bluffs of Memphis, seven miles away.

≈ V ≈

Journey's End

≈≈≈

In an instant the *Sultana* was mortally wounded and hundreds of her passengers were killed or crippled. The terrific force of the blast, in a furious updraft of destruction, hurled huge pieces of iron through the cabin, the hurricane deck, the texas and the pilothouse, tearing through the patchwork of bodies, splintering the midships area and virtually cutting the boat in two. Those who were sleeping immediately above the boilers were spewed straight up into the air as if from the mouth of a volcano, and their shattered bodies—whole or in fragments—rained back onto the stricken steamer along with a shower of broken boards. Many who lay on the rim of the volcano were thrown outward and landed in the river. Others by the score, somewhat farther removed from the spout, were scalded and maimed and buried under piles of rubble.

The resounding explosion was followed by an ear-splitting combination of other sounds—the crunching collapse of the stairways and portions of the hurricane deck, the crash of the toppling smokestacks, the clatter of falling wreckage, the hiss of escaping steam, the ominous crackle of burning wood, the hoarse shouts of men, the piercing screams of women and the crying of children.

Captain Elliott, asleep on the cot which the sergeant had found for him in the ladies' cabin, was jarred to consciousness by a report that sounded like a pack of artillery and a shock that felt like a railroad collision. Sitting upright, he strained his eyes into the Egyptian darkness and gasped for breath, his face, throat and lungs burning in a cloud of steam. With reeling mind, he listened to the shrieks, cries, prayers and groans.

Unable to shake off this terrible nightmare, he got to his feet, pulled on his clothing and made his way forward, groping along between the cots and the state-room doors, trying to avoid the frenzied crowd which was already dashing blindly about the cabin. Suddenly he discovered a broad opening in the deck. Uncertainly peering down into this hole, he could see a bed of red-hot coals some fifteen feet below. The fireboxes had been laid bare and the flames were running into the splintered hull, leaping into the chasm left by the departing boilers, quickly rising toward the decks above and lighting a scene of hellish horror.

As he stared down at the mangled, scalded human forms heaped amid the burning debris on the lower deck, Elliott heard a nearby voice—a voice which sounded remarkably calm and polite.

"Captain, will you please help me?"

It was Daniel McLeod, the Shiloh-crippled Illinois veteran who had boarded the *Sultana* at New Orleans. Five minutes earlier he had been reading at a table near the center of the cabin. When everyone nearer the bow had vanished into the crater, McLeod had been blown over the table with bone-fracturing violence. Now, as Elliott turned to face him, the captain saw that McLeod was sitting on the head of the cot nearest the breach. The cot was covered with pieces of the wreck, and McLeod was bruised, cut, scalded; both his ankles were broken and the bones showed through the torn skin. Using his suspenders, McLeod had already improvised tourniquets for both legs so that he would not bleed to death.

The cabin was thick with a suffocating mixture of smoke and steam which seared the eyes and made breathing difficult. "I'm powerless to help you," Elliott told him. "I can't swim." His words were almost lost in the bedlam of gasping, coughing, retching, running, shouting humanity.

"Throw me in the river is all I ask," replied McLeod in the same level tone. "I'll burn to death here."

Several yards away, through the hot, murky fog which was now alive with the dancing red of the flames, Elliott recognized a fellow Indianan, Captain Chapman of LaFayette, and called to him. Together the two officers lifted McLeod from the bunk, carried him out through the stern exit and dropped him into the river.

By this time a hot cloud was rolling and tumbling out of the remnant of the cabin, and from the gray-black vapors emerged a mob of passengers—screaming, praying, cursing—while the fire roared into an uncontrollable holocaust and bathed the *Sultana* in an eerie incandescence. Up on the hurricane deck Charles King was running through the crowd sobbing, "Oh, God! Oh, Mother! I am lost!" One of his bunkmates, George Downey, who had thought himself so lucky to get aboard at the coalyard, was dead. The other, Henry Kline, tried to follow King across the deck, but soon lost sight of him in the crowd.

Down on the main deck a man was perched on what was left of the first stairway, shouting over and over again at the top of his lungs, "The boat is sinking!" Howling terror seized the doomed *Sultana* and shook it, as a cat shakes a mouse. Years later the survivors recalled the sights and sounds: ". . . men who were scalded and bruised were crawling over one another to get out of the fire . . . it seemed as if some were coming out of the fire and from under the boiler . . . men who were buried beneath the wreck were crying for help . . . men caught in every conceivable manner . . . screaming in their agony . . . flames were madly rushing through the broken kindling of the boat cabin . . . the stench of burning flesh was intolerable."

In the black of night, confronted with such horror, the survivors of the explosion immediately began stampeding into the river. And the stampede was perhaps more deadly than the explosion itself.

". . . the heat was intense, driving the men back,

those in the center and nearest the fire crowding those on the outer edges into the river . . . men were trampling over each other in their endeavors to escape . . . the men rushed to the bow of the boat . . . to the stern . . . and jumped overboard as fast as they could, tumbling into the river upon each other and going down into the deep by the hundreds."

While the boat was taking on coal, A. C. Brown, the Ohio captain, had drifted off to sleep in his stateroom just aft of amidships. An hour later he awoke to find himself lying on the deck, on the opposite side of the cabin. Stunned and shaken, Brown saw that the stateroom which he had occupied was nothing more than a heap of splinters. In front of him a gaping hole was belching steam and smoke. Behind him the chandelier in the ladies' cabin was swinging crazily and still burning brightly. The captain picked himself up and joined the dash to the stern, passing a woman who was buckling a second life belt around a small child. At the rail he helped another woman throw her trunk into the river and saw her follow it. Then, after shedding his heavy army shirt, Brown jumped.

Farther toward the stern the explosion spent the last of its force on Stateroom Number 10, which was occupied by William Long of Leavenworth, Kansas. He awoke to find that the partition separating his room from the next room forward was splintered and full of holes, but the after partition was undamaged. Pulling on his shirt, Long left his trousers behind and raced to the stern only to discover that the boat was not near the bank. He hesitated and while wondering what to do, estimated that fifty persons jumped overboard every minute. After two or three minutes of watching the fire spread, he ran back to his stateroom, pulled on his pants, and returned to the stern where he dropped down to the main deck and climbed up on the taffrail. After another three or four hundred people had jumped into the river, Long finally decided to make his own leap, taking a door along to serve as a raft.

In one of the sternmost staterooms, near the ladies' cabin, Congressman-elect Snow was awakened by what he described as a shudder passing over the boat, but he didn't hear the explosion. Not knowing what had happened, he got up and began dressing. As he carefully adjusted his tie, he noticed steam seeping into the room. Opening the cabin door, he realized that the boilers had burst; the pilothouse and at least one-third of the cabin roof had fallen to the main deck. With the boat on fire and with a fresh breeze carrying the flames through the balance of the cabin toward the ladies' saloon, the heat was already oppressive. Snow knew that he would have to get off the *Sultana*. Turning back into his room, he removed his coat and tie, then trotted aft. The first frantic stampede through the cabin was past, and Snow stepped over several men, killed and trampled in the mad rush. From the rail, he saw that the water was a sea of heads, so close together that it was impossible to jump without landing on someone. After searching along the rail for some distance, he at last dropped into a tiny spot of open water near one of the paddle-wheel housings.

That night, as hundreds of *Sultana* passengers looked for a rescuer, there was only one other steamboat on the Mississippi between Memphis and Cairo—the new *Bostonia No.* 2, downward bound from Cincinnati, on her way to enter the Memphis and Natchez trade. At the time of the explosion, she was some twelve miles above the *Sultana,* and no one on board heard the blast. The *Bostonia*—namesake of the boat which had been destroyed by the exploding *Louisiana*—moved on unaware of the horror that lay ahead.

At Memphis, the U.S. military picket boat *Pocahontas* was lying at the foot of Beale Street. Shortly after two o'clock the boat's watchman noticed a bright light somewhere upriver and reported it to Henry Seman, the pilot, suggesting that it might be a farmhouse in flames. Seman watched the light grow brighter and concluded that a steamer was on fire, as he later boasted to a newspaper reporter, but he did nothing about it. And although dozens of people in the city would later insist that they had heard a booming sound at two o'clock in the morning, no one was curious enough to investigate.

At the tiny community of Mound City, Arkansas, some five miles above Memphis and two miles below the scene of the disaster, plantation-owner John Fogleman was awakened by the explosion. From his veranda he could see the glow of the burning steamer, and he aroused three of his neighbors, Thomas J. Lumbertson, George Malone and John Berry. The four men noticed that the light seemed to be moving downriver, getting closer. But only a handful of families—not more than six or eight—lived at Mound City, and not one of them kept a boat of any kind.

On the same side of the river and a little farther

upstream was a woodyard operated by William Boardman and R. K. Hill. These two men also heard the
explosion and saw the light from the fire, but it was
almost an hour before they heard screams and set out
in their skiff to see what was the matter.

In their battle against the fire and the flood, the
terror and the panic, the men, women and children of
the *Sultana* were alone. If they were to be saved, they
would have to save themselves.

Two factors weighed heavily against them. The
packet carried no lifeboats—in fact, no safety equipment of any sort, except for the cork life belts which
were racked beside or under each stateroom bed. More-
over, the explosion had occurred near mid-river. With
sizable islands scattered along both banks, Clayton,
the pilot, had been steering straight up the center
of the stream when the boilers burst. Unaware of this
fact, most of the passengers assumed that the boat
was within a few yards of the shore, as she had been
during much of the trip. Actually, the nearest land
was a matter of miles, not yards. Normally it would
have been a one-mile swim to the Arkansas bank and
twice that to the Tennessee side—even farther to the
islands astern. But both banks had vanished beneath
the overflow; only a ragged fringe of treetops marked
the usual borders of the river. Dry land was an elusive
fugitive hidden far back in the forest.

Whenever a riverboat exploded, the officers and
crew made every effort to run her aground so that the
passengers could escape onto shore. In the case of
the *Sultana*, however, such action was out of the question; the pilothouse was completely demolished, the

tiller rope was severed, and the boat became a drifting, uncontrollable hulk at the moment of the explosion.

If the fire had been brought under control, the passengers could have stayed on board until the vessel was carried to shore by the current. A few dozen buckets of water, promptly applied, would have quenched the fireboxes and choked off the blaze at its source. In spite of the general panic, a number of the soldiers quickly understood that putting out the fire was their best hope for survival. But in the surging crowd it was difficult to secure a foothold and impossible to search the dark decks for buckets or for lines to lower the buckets into the river. Within ten minutes the opportunity had passed; the blaze was out of control.

According to many of the survivors, Captain Cass Mason first tried to stop the stampede and then worked selflessly to save the drowning. Just after the explosion, Jacob Helminger of the 50th Ohio saw Mason on the hurricane deck, ordering the soldiers to wait, saying that the hull was not hurt and the *Sultana* would land. Helminger and others decided that Mason's plan would not work. The fire was the enemy, and it could not be defeated.

A few minutes later, according to J. W. Rush of the 95th Ohio, the captain, in his shirt sleeves and bareheaded, appeared on the boiler deck. Once again Mason tried to restore order, asking the crowd to quiet down and be patient. As he was speaking, a number of women came out of the cabin, knelt on the deck and, resting their heads against the stern rail, prayed for help.

Still later, on the main deck, C. M. Nisley, the commissary sergeant, joined in the futile effort to extinguish the fire and then, with Captain Mason, threw wreckage overboard for those already in the water. The fire finally became so hot that Nisley decided to take to the water. Captain Mason stayed on board. With his shattered packet blazing around him, he stood his deck to the last, working to save his passengers. No one reported seeing the captain leave the *Sultana,* and it can only be assumed that he and his steamer died together.

Of the three officers on duty at the time of the explosion, two were blown overboard, and the other was thrown into the flaming rubbish on the lower deck. Clemens, at his place of duty beside the boilers, was scalded from head to foot and hurled far out into the water. Rowberry and Clayton, standing only a few feet apart in the pilothouse, were tossed upward at slightly different angles. Rowberry, the mate, landed in the river, while Clayton, the pilot, came crashing down onto the main deck, half buried in the wreckage. Crawling out from under the remains of the pilothouse, Clayton tried to dissuade the passengers from jumping into the river, telling them to hold onto the wreck as long as possible. When his words went unheeded and the fire was clearly out of control, the pilot grabbed a plank and leaped like the rest.

Nathan Wintrenger, the chief engineer, was also tumbled onto the lower deck from his sleeping quarters in the texas. He stood bewildered for a moment, and then saw that the river was alive with passengers struggling in the water. The flames were spreading and Wintrenger quickly decided, because of the congestion and confusion, that there was no chance of halting the blaze. Convinced that he would soon be forced off anyway, he picked up a shutter and went over the rail.

At the moment that her boilers burst, the *Sultana* began mottling the river with victims. For several seconds, miniature geysers spouted on all sides as bodies plummeted down in a human hailstorm. Some of those who were blown overboard were too seriously injured to help themselves and immediately drowned; others came through the harrowing journey unscathed, except for the shock of awakening in the air or in the water.

Several men of the 102nd Ohio were sleeping on the boiler deck on the larboard side of the cabin, just inside the rail but outside of the balusters which supported the hurricane deck. Most of this group, including Joseph Bringman, P. L. Horn, John H. Kochenderfer and C. S. Schmutz, were catapulted into the river by the explosion.

Bringman, like most of the paroled prisoners, was weak and unwell. His sleep had been restless and disturbed by a dream—a dream mixed with reality: "It appeared to me in my dream that I was walking leisurely on an incline or sloping hill, and when I reached the top there appeared to be a ledge or projecting rock overhanging a river; I seemed to step upon it so as to look down into the water, and just as I took the second step the rock seemed to burst with a report like the shot of a distant cannon. I felt pieces of the rock striking my face and head and I seemed to be hurled out into the river. The sensation was like striking the water with my side and shoulder and going under with a waving or oscillating motion. I came to the surface, but was still not fully conscious. With apparently the same motion, I started to go down again, but did not seem to go down so far. I became more conscious and began to struggle." It was not now a dream. Bringman soon found his clothing an encumbrance and quickly undressed. Coming to the surface, he struck a scantling some four inches square, seized it and also managed to get some more debris, which kept him afloat.

In addition to the men in the water near him, Bringman saw horses struggling to swim, and one of them nearly capsized his frail float. In a short time the flames of the *Sultana* lighted up the river and Bringman could see that for a distance of two hundred yards from the boat, the water was covered with people; some swimming boldly, others floundering and grasping at any object, human or otherwise, which offered hope of support.

Schmutz was aroused from slumber by a "burning and falling sensation." Finding himself in mid-air, he had time to shout, "What's the matter?" before dropping into the water. His first thought was that he had somehow rolled under the rail and fallen overboard. Being a good swimmer, he set out in pursuit of the boat, but soon discovered that he was not alone in the river, and moments later he saw the boat catch fire. In a state of shock, he grasped a piece of wreckage and floated away, every now and then ducking his head to cool his scalded face.

Horn also awoke to find that he was "lost in the air," and the next moment he was lost in the water. Rising to the surface, he bumped into a piece of wreckage, and with seven others, he clung to this welcome support, apparently a section of the boiler-deck guardrail, about seven inches wide and twenty feet long.

Kochenderfer heard nothing and felt nothing. He simply opened his eyes and discovered that he was "about three hundred feet from the boat, shrouded in total darkness and in what appeared to be an ocean of water." After recovering from his surprise, he calmly turned on his back and floated downstream, "in a position to see the stern and one side of the boat where hundreds were dropping off into the river, and most of them going to their death."

Another of the human projectiles was Perry Summerville, the Indiana lad who had burned his crutches at Cahaba. He was thrown, by his own calculation, at least one hundred feet. Believing that the *Sultana* had been hugging the bank and that he had been knocked overboard by a tree limb, Summerville, very much excited, began to swim toward the boat, calling for help. Soon, however, he could see fire and steam and hear the screams of those on board, and so he began swimming slowly away, occasionally looking back in wonder at the burning steamer.

One sizable section of the boiler deck was blown into the river intact, complete with the men who were sleeping on it. Among the unwilling riders was Jotham W. Maes of the 47th Ohio. With a teeth-rattling jar the unorthodox aircraft hit the water, scattering the men in all directions. As Maes splashed his way back to the piece of wreckage, in company with nine others, he glanced back at the *Sultana*. The smokestacks were lying crisscross, crushing everyone they had struck. The boat was on fire and the flames were driving men into the water by the hundred. No matter how good a swimmer a man might be, if he was in one of the crowds, he was doomed to go down with the clutching mass.

The packet's huge paddle-wheel housings, though loosened by the explosion, remained attached to the boat for a time. While they did—for the better part of an hour—the hull drifted stern first, since the housings acted as sails and kept the bow pointing into a brisk wind out of the north. During this brief interval, as the flame-wrapped wreck slipped backward with the current, hundreds of private life-and-death dramas were played in the flickering firelight.

On the main deck . . .

Albert W. King, John Davis, George Hill, William Wheeler and Adgate Fleming of the 100th Ohio were bunking together about thirty feet from the stern, inside the engine-room partition. "We had slept about an hour when the crash came," wrote King. "Men, coal, wood and timbers from the boat were thrown over and beyond us. The steam and ashes smothered us so we could scarcely breathe. Several seconds passed before I recovered sufficiently to know what had happened. When I came to my senses, I rushed for the stern entrance, falling several times before I reached the fresh air. My four companions were soon by my side, having also escaped any serious injury from the explosion."

Buffeted by the milling crowd, King and his friends went to work on the stern end of the partition, trying to break off a large piece of siding to use as a float. They had almost succeeded when a fear-crazed, rearing horse tied to the after rail drove them away. Meanwhile, Fleming pleaded with the others to tell him what to do; he couldn't swim. Shouting above the noise, King repeatedly warned him to stay close and to keep out of the crowd at the rail. But when the group was driven away from the siding, Fleming rushed into the mob and was carried overboard and drowned.

In the bedlam, King soon became separated from Davis, Hill and Wheeler. Unable to find anything that would float, but afraid to remain on the burning boat, he climbed the starboard rail and leaped as far as possible. Bobbing up near the rudder, he was ducked several times by drowning men. Exhausted, he glimpsed an opening through the crowd and was swimming desperately to escape when someone jumped on him from above and carried him under again. No sooner had he regained the surface than a floundering woman grabbed him by the shirt. Frantically, King fought free and swam away, but finding a board moments later, he returned to the woman and gave his help. With King paddling and kicking, the pair and their plank moved away from the boat, out of the crowded circle of firelight into the night.

Two Kentuckians rushed to the taffrail and stared down at the sinking swarm, each telling the other that he could not swim. "Then let's die together," one of them said. They jumped and were swallowed by the river.

A woman with a two-month-old baby in her arms made her way down from her stateroom on the second deck. Crying with fear, she went up to a soldier at the stern and asked for help.

The soldier told her, "It's everyone for himself."

As he spoke he noticed that her life preserver was too low on her waist, and he reached to unbuckle it.

"Soldier," she said, "don't take that off from me."

"It must be up under your arms," he said.

He pulled the belt into proper position and refastened it. Then he took the woman by the arm, escorted her to the stern and helped her onto the guard.

"May the Lord bless you," she said. With the baby held tightly in her arms, she stepped off the rail.

Absalom N. Hatch of the 1st Michigan Engineers and Mechanics was bedded down on the coils of line which lay near the jack staff, on the very tip of the bow. So quickly did the stampede follow the explosion that several men ran over him before he could scramble to his feet. A few minutes later he followed them, carrying an oak scantling.

Patrick Larky of the 18th Michigan was pushed off the bow and struggled unsuccessfully to keep his head above water. He tried to climb onto a small board, but it slipped out of his grasp. As he went under he screamed, "Come help poor Pat, he is a-drowning!" But the plea went unanswered, and the Irishman disappeared.

Simeon Chelf, lying against one of the cable posts, was awakened by a piece of iron glancing off his head. Only a month earlier, as a member of General James Wilson's "Lightning Brigade," Chelf had ridden into

Alabama on the last offensive of the war, to destroy the Confederate arsenal at Selma. Along with several other members of his regiment, the 6th Kentucky Cavalry, he had been captured near Tuscaloosa on April 1, and had almost immediately been brought to the Big Black River for exchange.

Now, his head aching, Chelf crawled out from under his blankets. Avoiding the rush he picked up a board about fifteen feet long and waited for an opportunity to jump. A. M. Jacobs, another of Wilson's Kentucky troopers, approached with a small pole which he wanted to give Chelf in exchange for the board, explaining, "You can swim and I can't." Chelf agreed to the trade and told him, "I'll help you all I can, but a man can't do much in water." The two men went to the point of the bow; found there were too many men in the water, and decided to remain on board as long as possible.

Ogilvie E. Hamblin of the 2nd Michigan Cavalry was near the forward entrance to the cargo hold and awoke to hear men inside screaming for someone to open the hatch. Hamblin had been wounded in the shoulder and captured by Hood's horsemen at Raccoon Ford on the Tennessee River in October. Soon after, the Rebel doctors at Florence, Alabama, had amputated his injured arm, according to Hamblin, "for practice." Now, needing help to pull the heavy hatch cover away, he called to his friend Frank Perkins. Together the two shoved the crowd off the hatch and swung it back. Instantly the men below "came rushing out of the hold like bees out of a hive, followed by dense clouds of steam and smoke."

Hamblin stripped down to the skin and remained on board for some time, watching the men struggling in the river. But as the fire drew closer, he knew that he must jump. "Screwing my courage up to the sticking point," he wrote, "I prepared to take the leap into the icy waters which I expected to be my sepulchre. I watched my chance for a clear spot so that no one would catch onto me and drown me at once. Into the water, and when I arose to the surface I struck out as best I could. Having but one arm to swim with, I found I could do nothing against the strong current, and so let myself float down with the current."

Chester Berry was sleeping forward of the boilers, near the spot where he had sung his hymn at sundown. A flying piece of wood from the engine-room partition struck his head, fracturing his skull. Dazed and bewildered, he did not get up until a shower of boiling water began soaking through his blanket. Then he discovered that the blanket had probably saved his life; his bunkmate, who had lain beside him uncovered, had been scalded to death.

Berry grabbed a small board and started forward, but when he reached the bow and looked down, he changed his mind about jumping: "I came to the conclusion I did not want to take to the water just then, for it was literally black with human beings, many of whom were sinking and taking others with them. Being a good swimmer and having board enough to save me even if I were not, I concluded to wait till the rush was over."

While he waited, Berry roamed the deck, hoping to find a friend. Amid the tumult and uproar he came across a man who was crying and wringing his hands, apparently in great pain, loudly wailing, "Oh dear! Oh dear!" Berry asked the man if he were badly injured.

"I'm not hurt at all, but I can't swim. I've got to drown. Oh dear!"

Doing his best to calm the man, Berry showed him the board he carried. "There, do you see that? Now you go to that pile of broken deck and get you one like it, and when you jump, put it under your chin and you can't drown."

"But I did get one, and someone snatched it away from me."

"Well then, get another."

"I did, and they took that away from me."

"Well then, get another."

"Why, what would be the use? They would take it away from me. Oh dear, I tell you there's no use. I've got to drown. I can't swim."

Berry's fractured skull was aching and throbbing and his patience was exhausted. He gave the hysterical man a shove and walked away, storming at him, "Drown then, you fool!" For the rest of his life Berry, who became a preacher, carried the incident on his conscience.

On the boiler deck . . .

Captain Elliott pushed his way back into the smoke-filled cabin, entered an empty stateroom and found a life preserver. While he was making his way back to the stern exit, a frightened young woman in her nightgown ran past him. He followed her outside and seized her arm as she was mounting the rail. Calling to the chambermaid—the Victorian proprieties had to be observed—Elliott saw his life belt fastened about the woman's waist and watched her plunge overboard.

Nearby, the younger Safford fastened two life belts on his father, the Christian Commissioner, and one on himself. They jumped together and climbed on a stateroom door, which they had thrown into the water before them. But as they tried to paddle away from the stern, a horse leaped from the main deck and struck the door. In the confusion and the crowd, the two men became separated.

"I saw a woman rush out of a stateroom in her night-clothes with a little child in her arms," wrote William McFarland. "In a moment she had fastened a life preserver about its waist and then threw it overboard. The preserver had evidently been fastened on too low, for when the little one hit the water it turned wrong end up. The mother rushed into the stateroom an instant and was then out and sprang into the water and grabbed the child—all of which occurred in the space of a couple of minutes."

William Boor of the 64th Ohio, who had thought at Vicksburg that the boilers did not look very safe, was pinned down by a section of the upper deck which had collapsed under a falling smokestack. Wriggling free of the rubble, he cleared the broken timbers away from his messmate, Thomas Brink. As the pair worked their way down the wrecked stairway, Boor asked, "Can you swim?" and Brink replied that he could. Boor admitted that he could not, but promised to meet his friend somewhere on shore. The reunion, however, never took place. On reaching the bow, Brink immediately dived overboard and was never seen again. Boor, being afraid of the water and the grasping crowd, could not muster enough courage to jump. Returning to the boiler deck, he tied his spare shirt in a rubber blanket and picked up a loose piece of wood. With the bundle and the board tucked under his arms, he again made his way to the bow and waited indecisively between fire and flood.

W. A. Huld of the 64th Ohio, sleeping near the head of the first stairway, was "awakened by a terrible crash and nearly smothered by hot steam." With considerable difficulty, he groped his way down the dark stairway, past the man who stood on its lower end shouting, "The boat is sinking." As he pressed on toward the bow, he passed the wooden cover which Hamblin and Perkins had pulled away from the cargo hatch. Picking it up, Huld carried it to the forward rail and dropped it into the water. He leaped after it, but three men seized his raft and got away with it. However, Huld used the space left by the three men and escaped the dangerous mob near the *Sultana*.

L. W. McCrory of the 100th Ohio was lying a few feet away from Huld's sleeping place, next to the stairway which curved up to the hurricane deck. When the forward end of the promenade collapsed, McCrory would have been crushed, had it not been for the stair banister. As the snapped timbers came crashing down, the banister caught the wreckage and stopped its fall a bare foot above his body. Sliding out from under the debris, McCrory searched about until he found his valise, which contained a good suit of civilian clothes, and his heavy iron-bound pocketbook, which contained a hundred dollars. With these two possessions clutched to his chest, he climbed the boiler-deck rail and crawled out onto a small gangplank tackled to the gin pole.

Astride the narrow plank for fifteen minutes or more, he waited until flames burned close. Then cautiously he stood up, put his pocketbook between his teeth, gripped his valise tightly in one hand and jumped into the water eighteen feet below. Although the pocketbook kept his mouth partially open, forcing him to swallow a quantity of water, he held on doggedly until he came to the surface. Refusing to become excited, he took the pocketbook in his free hand, and with the valise still clutched in the other, he set out awkwardly for the Arkansas bank.

On the hurricane deck . . .

Ben Davis of the 7th Kentucky Cavalry was restless after the boat left the coalyard and decided to have a smoke. It was a long, difficult walk from the hurricane deck down to the boiler deck and then down to the main deck, but there was no other way to get a light for his pipe. Slowly he made his way across the patchwork of bodies and down the stairways. Poking a splinter into one of the fireboxes, he sucked the flame into his pipe and retraced his steps. Back on the hurricane deck he puffed contentedly for several minutes, then rapped the ashes out of the bowl and felt for his canteen. As he lifted the metal container toward his lips it was wrenched from his hand by the explosion and whirled away into the night.

To Davis it appeared that "the boat had all gone to pieces." He had been sharing blankets with three friends from Cahaba—John Andorf, Joe Moss and Morris Malachy. But the four men became separated, and Davis slid down a line to the main deck. With the fire snapping and crackling overhead, he searched for something that would float. Just as he picked up a window shutter about three feet square, Joe Moss appeared. Moss begged for the shutter, pleading that he could not swim. The two men went to the rail, where Davis threw the shutter into the water and told Moss to jump after it. Without a word, Moss went over the side and vanished forever. Davis slipped out of his trousers and shoes and plunged into the river, making for the Arkansas bank.

A. A. Jones of the 115th Ohio, lying between Martin Baird and Robert Gaylord, was covered by wreckage. After a struggle he extricated himself and found that his companions had both been crushed to death. By the time Jones reached the rail, the water below was lighted by the fire. With cold horror he watched the "masses of drowning men clinging together until they were borne down by their own weight to rise no more alive." Even thirty years later, their "poor, pinched and ghastly faces" were deeply engraved on his memory. Letting himself down to the main deck on a line, Jones secured a plank and took to the water. At first he tried to stay as near the boat as possible, but he was soon forced to swim away to avoid being struck by the shower of boards, barrels and boxes being thrown overboard.

Hugh Kinser and John Carr of the 50th Ohio made their way down to the main deck, into the pandemonium. Seizing a small slat, Carr shouted, "I'm going to try to get out of this," and vaulted the rail. Kinser peered out into the night and watched his companion drown. Then he steeled himself to make his own attempt at escape. Although wasted by a four-month confinement at Cahaba, he was a good swimmer and decided to take his chances. Springing into the water, he swam a few yards, but his strength deserted him so fast that he turned back. A line to which two or three poor fellows were clinging, hung by the side of the boat. Kinser caught onto it and climbed above them. Gradually the hold of those below him weakened and they sank into the deep water. Kinser's own grasp was failing, and he was sliding down the same way the others had done when a large board came floating by. With an effort Kinser threw himself on it, and the next instant someone jumped on top of him and said, "Shove out of here." Kinser did, and the two managed to steer clear of others who were desperately grasping at anything within reach. One more on the board would have meant death.

Charlie King, still wailing, "I am lost," scrambled over the railing and dropped into the water below. His company commander, Lieutenant Swain, followed him into the river. Swain, an excellent swimmer, succeeded in getting the boy onto a plank and spoke to him comfortingly. "Don't cry so," he said. "I'll take you out safely." King immediately stopped sobbing and said not another word. Swain swam behind, pushing plank and rider before him.

Truman Smith, the young cavalryman who had been captured at Henryville, Tennessee, and Henry Norton, another member of the 8th Michigan Cavalry, met on the shattered deck. Norton was furious. His bundle of clothes had been stolen and he swore that he would shoot the thief. Smith told him to forget it and get ready to swim, but Norton felt there was plenty of time for that. It would take only a few minutes to reach the bank, he said, and he had no intention of leaving until he found the scoundrel who had stolen his clothes. While Norton continued his search, Smith went into the river with an empty barrel, but soon discovered that the barrel, having only one head, rolled and tumbled and could not be managed. He lost the barrel and then almost lost his life: "I started to swim but found that someone had hold of me and I could not get loose. We had a struggle in the water and I freed myself by giving him my blouse. The night was dark and I could not see which way to go. I swam but a few feet when I found myself with four or five others. It seemed as though we all wanted to get hold of each other. I succeeded in getting the rest of my clothes off and got rid of my company."

Sergeant Joseph Stevens, the Michigan Sharpshooter with the Yorkshire accent, and his brother-in-law William Finch, whom he had met unexpectedly at Camp Fisk, were near the stern when the *Sultana* exploded. Finch quickly became hysterical with fear because he could not swim and Stevens tried to reason with him, telling him that he could not swim either, but that they still might escape if they kept their senses. Finch paid no attention. Breaking away from his brother-in-law's grasp he ran aft toward the yawl hanging over the stern, customary equipment on sidewheel packets. Stevens screamed at him to come back. The small boat was already full—too full—of desperate men. Tugging at the tackle, trying to lower them-

The wharf at Vicksburg where more than two thousand **Union** soldiers were hurried aboard the *Sultana*.

All the soldiers wanted to be in this photograph, taken at Helena, Arkansas, the day before the *Sultana* exploded.

Some of the survivors
as they appeared
in 1890.

Captain A. C. Brown's friends
wanted him to be comfortable.

Sergeant Joseph Stevens had a
touch of Yorkshire in his speech.

Private Perry S. Summerville
burned his crutches and
lost his cane.

Private Samuel H. Raudebaugh
tried to get on the icebox.

Sergeant Jacob Helminger didn't
believe the *Sultana's* captain.

Private Chester Berry sang softly
at the vesper hour.

Private Otto Bardon was willing
to guide a trunk.

Private Joseph Bringman floated
past the Memphis water front.

Lieutenant George B. McCord
carefully rode a foot-plank.

Corporal Simeon Chelf made a
generous exchange.

Captain J. Walter Elliott decided
to use his cousin's name.

Sergeant William Fies found a
useful sapling.

The Old Army Game.

Major General Cadwallader C. Washburn broke the seal on a new deck of cards.

Secretary of War Edwin M. Stanton played a brief hand.

Brigadier General William Hoffman eliminated some of the players.

Major General N. J. T. Dana was among the winners.

Perhaps other players are in this carefully composed photograph of the last exchange at Camp Fisk in April, 1865.

The last of the *Sultana* as seen in a vivid woodcut which appeared in *Harper's Weekly*.

The New-York Times.

NEW-YORK, SATURDAY, APRIL 29, 1865.

DREADFUL DISASTER.

Explosion of a Mississippi Steamer—Fourteen Hundred Lives Supposed to be Lost—They are Nearly all Released Union Prisoners—A Terrible Responsibility Resting upon Somebody.

ST. LOUIS, Friday, April 28.

A telegram received by the military authorities from New-Madrid says that the steamer *Sultana*, with two thousand paroled prisoners, exploded. Fourteen hundred lives were lost.

SECOND DISPATCH.

CAIRO, Friday, April 28.

The steamer *Sultana*, from New-Orleans the evening of the 21st, arrived at Vicksburgh with boilers leaking badly. She remained twenty hours repairing, taking on 1,996 Federal soldiers, and thirty-five officers, lately released from Cahawba and Andersonville prisons. She arrived at Memphis last evening, and after coaling proceeded. About 2 A. M., when seven miles up, blew up and immediately took fire and burned to the water's edge. Of 2,106 souls aboard, not more than 780 will be recovered. Five hundred were rescued, and are now in the hospitals. Two or three hundred, uninjured, are at the Soldiers' Home. Capt. MASON, of the *Sultana*, is supposed to be lost. At 4 o'clock this morning the river in front of Memphis was covered with soldiers struggling for life. Many are badly scalded. Boats immediately went to their rescue, and are still engaged picking them up. Gen. WASHBURN immediately organized a board of officers to investigate the affair. They are now at work.

No further particulars are received.

The story of the greatest marine disaster of all time was quickly forgotten by the press. The first story in the New York *Times* was a five-inch item on page four. Before dropping the story, the *Times* gave less than two columns to it.

selves into the water, the occupants were mercilessly beating off the berserk crowd trying to get aboard. Unexpectedly the lines let go and the boat hurtled down, turning over as it fell, and landing on the heads of those who had been spilled into the water, trapping them underneath. The crowd on deck then cascaded into the water to continue the deadly fight for possession. When it was over, only a handful clung to the edges of the overturned craft which had caused the death of scores. William Finch was among the lost.

Sergeant Stevens jumped over the rail and was floundering helplessly when his friend, Charles Taber, heard him scream and recognized his voice. Taber was floating on a bale of hay nearby, and he immediately swam to the rescue, grabbed Stevens by the hair and pulled him onto the float. Gasping and coughing, Stevens looked back at the boat, and on the second deck he saw Captain Mason tearing off window shutters and throwing them into the river for the boys.

W. A. Fast of the 102nd Ohio, after watching the fight for the yawl, made his way down to the boiler deck and unsuccessfully searched the staterooms for a life belt. Forward, where the decking had been broken off, he watched the men below rushing out and pouring over the prow into the dark water like a flock of sheep through a gap in a fence. Fast heard the men standing on the debris and on the edge of the boat praying, singing and swearing a blue streak. Some cursed Abe Lincoln, Jeff Davis, General Grant—anybody and everybody prominently connected with the war. Some were crying like children. Some were praying very loudly and passionately, while others "were getting off very formal and graceful prayers—all in dead earnest."

Fast, by contrast, kept his composure and made careful preparations for his venture into the river. He pried off a stateroom door, carried it to the edge of the jagged hole made by the explosion, and after watching the men around him for a few minutes, he dropped the door onto the wreckage which covered the lower deck and jumped down. When the first wild stampede was over, Fast took the door and made his way forward to the bow. Pulling down fifteen or twenty feet of line from the jack staff, he carefully tied it to the door, leaving several loops to serve as handles when the door was in the water. A few burly deck hands were still on board, crazed with excitement and fear, and they grabbed at Fast's carefully prepared raft—the best buoy then in sight—and tried to wrench it from his grasp. To save it, Fast walked back to the stairway, wedged the door between some timbers, took out a small jackknife and stood to defend his possession.

As the crowd thinned out, Fast stripped off his trousers, and then, with the flames roaring overhead, he again made his way forward. Calmly looking at a small open-faced watch which was tied to his drawers, he noted that the time was half past two. He threw his door into the water, jumped in after it and was soon afloat. Almost immediately a soldier took hold of the door, then another and another, and soon half a dozen were struggling for possession. Fast was the strongest at first and he wrenched one hand after another from his float, but soon he became exhausted. Within twenty minutes he lost the door, and along with the door he lost his power of memory. From the time he was separated from the raft until daylight, his life was a blank and, although he was saved, he could never remember where he had been or what he had done during those hours in the river.

Between the head of the second stairway and the forward edge of the hurricane deck, there was sleeping room for just four men—William Wendt, John P. Day and John Kiney, all of the 8th Michigan Cavalry, and George Meade of the 21st Michigan. Wendt was awakened by a shower that fell from the condensing steam. Jumping up, he looked around for the pranksters who were throwing water. Then hearing someone scream "Fire!" Wendt awakened his friends. Kiney and Meade scrambled to their feet, stumbled backward and with flailing arms fell silently into the river. Both were drowned. Wendt and Day made their separate ways downstairs, and after each had secured a plank, one jumped from the bow and one from the stern.

George Robinson, the 2nd Michigan Cavalry's escape artist, didn't hear the explosion, probably because he was stunned. The first thing he remembered was someone calling, "For God's sake, cut the deck, I'm burning to death." Slowly Robinson realized that he was in the coal and that the deck on which he had been sleeping was on top of him. His arms were scalded and the hot steam was so thick he could hardly breathe. When he saw his partner, John Corliss, lying dead across his legs, Robinson gave up hope. Then he heard someone say, "Jack, you can get out this way." His next memory was of someone putting a hand on his shoulder and saying, "What will I do? I can't swim?" Robinson looked around and saw three or four hundred men in a solid mass in the water, all trying to get on top. But that was not the worst sight; there were men, fast in the wreckage, burning to death. The screaming and yelling were, for Robinson, never to be forgotten. All he could do was to work his way forward to the bow, sit down and wrap one arm around the jack staff.

Three-quarters of the texas was completely demolished by the explosion, and one of the smokestacks fell across the quarter that remained. Of the ten men who were inside at the time, only Mason and Wintrenger got out alive. Ingram, the second pilot; Butler, the second mate; Gamble and Stratton, the clerks; McGinty and O'Hara, the barkeepers; and Cross and Slater, the stewards, were all killed instantly.

Most of the soldiers sleeping on the roof above—on the texas deck—shared the fate of the boat's luckless officers. Twelve or fifteen were there, and only three escaped. Stephen Gaston, the fifteen-year-old who had been eating sugar two hours earlier, worked his way out of the wreckage. After an unsuccessful search for his friend Block, he swung down to the boiler deck on the breeching of the stack and jumped from the starboard rail. C. J. Lahue of the 13th Indiana was tumbled overboard, but he managed to catch onto the hurricane-deck railing and hung there for several minutes before dropping into the water. William H. Peacock of the 9th Indiana was tossed down through the chasm onto the main deck and was forced to work his way out from under the boards and bodies which fell on top of him. Peacock weighed only ninety-one pounds; he had lost more than 100 pounds since his capture at Athens seven months earlier. After a nightmarish struggle, he came crawling out of the pile—his shoulder cut and bleeding, his back bruised and his right side and hip badly scalded—an emaciated youngster in his underwear, with a hat still on his head and a handkerchief—the parting gift of a friend who had died at Vicksburg—knotted about his neck. Never pausing, Peacock crawled straight off the side of the boat.

From the heights of the splintered promenade to the depths of the flooded river—under the heavy pall of smoke which flared out umbrellalike above the disintegrating steamer—the seething mass contended for life, savagely, and with few heroics.

While some hundred or more on the hurricane deck were battling for possession of the yawl—most of them losing their lives in the process—others on the main deck were fighting to escape on the gangplank. Immediately after the explosion, men began hacking at the lines that held the big portable ramp suspended high above the starboard quarter. At length the pulleys squealed into motion as the frayed rope ends whipped through the tackle, and the heavy burden came crashing down, killing a number of soldiers who were standing underneath. The moment the gangplank hit the deck, a swarm gathered about it like ants around a cake crumb. In spite of the gangplank's size and weight—six feet wide, forty feet long and heavily ironbound—it was hoisted into the air. From one side of the boat to the other, the lurching, stumbling crowd tried to shove their prize into the water.

James K. Brady and David Ettleman of the 64th Ohio arrived from the hurricane deck just in time to participate in the launching. Brady had awakened to find his friend Ettleman brushing out a fire that had already burned most of the hair off Brady's head. As soon as the fire was out, the two began searching for a way to escape. Finding nothing on the hurricane deck, they slid down a line to the bow, where the savage survivors were trampling the bodies of the dead. A crowd was struggling with the gangplank, and the two men caught onto the ramp just as it went over the side. Forty or fifty men were on the plank as it struck the water, end first. Brady thought it would never stop going down, but finally it did, then slowly rose to the surface. Only fifteen or sixteen had stuck to the plank, among them Brady and Ettleman.

Someone seized Brady by the right foot with the strength of a vise, and gripping the plank with all his strength, Brady at last succeeded in prying the stranger loose with his left foot. By this time the gangplank had turned over and more of its passengers were gone. Brady looked back and saw that there were two men holding onto the plank behind him, and he could hear Ettleman in front of him shouting encouragement. The two men behind crawled up on top of the plank and upset it for the second time. One of the men let go and went down forever; the other was so terrified that he not only climbed on the plank again, but also reached over and tried to grab Brady by the shoulder. Just as the clawing fingers touched his shirt, Brady dropped under water and the soldier went over him into the river, turning the plank with the force of his plunge. Brady came up on the other side of the plank, catching it with his left hand, but the frightened man was never seen again.

Brady, who weighed only ninety-six pounds, was now nearly exhausted. Almost ready to give up, he heard Ettleman say, "Boys, this plank is able to carry fifteen or twenty men if properly handled, and there are only five or six of us. Now, I'll steady the plank while the rest of you get on and lie flat. Then I'll get on."

Ettleman's plan worked, and the men cautiously climbed aboard. Lying on their stomachs, each paddled with one arm, some on one side and some on the other. In addition to Brady and Ettleman, the party of survivors included Henry Gambill of the 14th Kentucky, Nicholas Karns of the 18th Ohio and no more than two others. Only these few were saved by the huge gangplank which had once offered hope to so many.

Most of those who escaped from the *Sultana* did it, not by stampeding blindly into the river, or by playing follow-the-leader after the yawl, or by joining the mob that seized the gangplank. They did it by thinking and acting independently. In the midst of a panic, when death is near, such men are rare. On board the *Sultana* one of the rarest of these was William Lugenbeal of the 135th Ohio, a twenty-year-old private captured at North Mountain, West Virginia, in June of '64.

Lugenbeal had already demonstrated his resourcefulness at Andersonville. Faced with starvation in the stockade, he had managed to get outside by volunteering to work with a construction crew, building a half-dozen storage sheds on the south side of the compound. From the place where he was quartered, near the railroad depot, he had been allowed to wander a mile without a guard and as a result, his weight had risen from an even one hundred pounds to one hundred and sixty-five—a fact which he attributed to stealing sweet potatoes and peanuts.

On the *Sultana*, engulfed by a terrible roar and crash while sleeping on the boiler deck, Lugenbeal discovered that his bunkmate, Joseph Test, had been killed by a piece of timber which was driven completely through his body. Hurrying down to the main deck, Lugenbeal took in the situation and immediately thought of a way to get ashore.

The alligator!

Lugenbeal walked to the closet beneath the stairway, kicked open the door and dragged the big box outside. Dumping the hissing reptile onto the deck, he ran his bayonet through it three times. Then removing all of his outer clothing, he dragged the box to the bow and threw it overboard. After some difficulty he at last pulled himself into this private lifeboat; the sides fitted snugly under his armpits and he dangled his legs over one end, so that he could paddle with his hands and kick with his feet at the same time.

Propelling himself downstream, Lugenbeal worked industriously to repulse the desperate: "When a man would get close enough I would kick him off, then turn quick as I could and kick someone else to keep them from getting hold of me." Occasionally a man would call, "Don't kick, I'm drowning!" But Lugenbeal observed matter-of-factly, "If they had got hold of me, we would both have drowned." And to those who later heard the story, he posed the disturbing question: "What do you think you would do?"

Most of the able-bodied and active were so panic-stricken or so preoccupied with their own escape that they paid no attention to the pleas of the wounded and trapped. In fact, the screams merely served to increase the panic and put spurs to the stampede. Only here and there, now and then, was any effort made to rescue doomed men, and all too often the attempt was a failure.

"For God's sake, someone help me get this man out!"

The shout came from a strapping lieutenant on the main deck—an officer of a Kentucky regiment whom the soldiers called "Big Kentuck." He was bending over the frantically wriggling figure of a man held fast by a timber lying across his feet. M. C. White of the 8th Michigan Cavalry heard the shout and joined the struggle to free the man. Even together, they could not release him; soon he was roasted by the intense heat.

Five Ohioans of the 95th—George H. Young, W. F. Clancy, S. Muller and two others—were sleeping halfway between the cabin and the staircase when the boilers burst. Two of the men were crushed to death by the end of the hurricane deck, while Young, Clancy and Muller were pinned under the wreckage. Hearing shouts for help, a soldier on the roof of the cabin scrambled down and broke away the boards which held Clancy. And Clancy, in turn, succeeded in releasing Young.

Together they tried to free Muller, but he was caught by a beam so heavy that the two men could not budge it. While they were tugging at the weight, a gust of wind blew the flames directly into their faces, and they were forced to retreat. As soon as the flames were billowed away, they ran back to Muller and desperately bent their backs against the timber. Again the flames drove them away. From the rail Young and Clancy listened helplessly to Muller's agonized cries and pleas and both could only feel a sense of relief when death ended his suffering.

By the time Young and Clancy made their way down to the main deck, the fire was raging overhead and most of the soldiers had fled to the bow or stern, leaving the injured behind. Overcome by fear, Clancy began babbling. Twice Young stopped him from jumping, pointing out that the water was full of drowning men, but at last, with the fire sweeping forward, Clancy ran to the side and went over the rail.

Soon the heat became so intense that Young could not stay in the mid-section of the boat, and he could see no chance of getting beyond the burning wreckage to the bow or stern. So he picked up a rubber blanket —the only thing he could find—and threw it onto the water. When he jumped, the blanket kept him from going under.

A half hour after the explosion, it was obvious that the entire boat, including everything and everyone aboard, would be consumed by the fire within a matter of minutes. It was equally plain that no rescuer was going to arrive in time to remove the hundreds of survivors who still remained on the flaming wreck. They would have to take their chances in the river or burn to death. The choice was clear and unavoidable; it could not be long delayed.

On all three decks the wounded begged to be thrown overboard, preferring to drown rather than roast. And on each deck there were a few men with stomach enough for the job. M. H. Sprinkle and Billy Lockhart of the 16th Ohio threw at least fifty helpless soldiers over the hurricane-deck rail; Captain Elliott and a few others worked on the boiler deck, amid the ruins of the cabin; down on the main deck Private Commodore Smith of the 18th Michigan faced up to what he called "the hardest task of my life."

Ever since the explosion, Smith had been praying that another steamboat would happen along, but at last he realized that the prayer was not to be answered, at least not in time. So, with the help of several companions, he grimly set about the chore that had to be done: "When at length the last shadow of hope had expired . . . we proceeded to perform, carefully but hurriedly, the most heartrending task that human beings could be called upon to perform—that of throwing overboard into the jaws of certain death those comrades who were unable to help themselves. Some were so badly scalded by the hot water and steam from the exploded boilers that the flesh was falling from their bones." Smith heard their last prayers, received their thanks, dropped them over the side, saw them writhe in the muddy water, listened to their dying groans and watched them sink out of sight. Finally he followed them into the river.

After doing everything possible for the wounded, Elliott also began making preparations for his own escape: "I now cast about me for something I could use as a buoy, but everything available seemed to have been appropriated. I tried to improvise a life preserver out of a stool. I threw a mattress overboard. It floated and was at once caught onto by several who were struggling in the water. I got another mattress, and slipping down a fender onto the taffrail I dropped it, but it no sooner touched the water than four men seized it, turned it over, and it went under as I jumped. Down, down I went into the chilly waters. Some poor drowning wretch was clutching at my legs, but putting my hands down to release myself and vigorously treading water, I rose strangling to the surface, my scalded throat and lungs burning with pain. The mattress was within reach, with only one claimant. God only knows what had become of the three others."

Lockhart jumped from the hurricane deck.

Sprinkle was also heading for the rail, when he noticed Charles Ogden, a private of his company, who appeared to be dazed and unaware of his surroundings. Sprinkle shouted at him, "You've got to get off, Charlie, or you'll burn!" Ogden neither saw nor heard him and Sprinkle felt the deck trembling beneath his feet. With a sprint he hurdled the rail and slammed into the water twenty feet below. By the time he bobbed up, the hurricane deck had collapsed in a shower of sparks.

Chester Berry, after jumping from the main deck,

had been in the water only a few minutes when he heard a grinding of wood. Looking back he saw the hurricane deck let go, and at the same moment he saw a man leap from the falling deck onto one of the paddle-wheel housings, but the housing, too, was almost eaten away by the fire. The man sank halfway through the weakened planks and there he remained, stuck fast. Thirty rods away, Berry could plainly hear the man's blood-chilling screams as he was enveloped by the blue, curling flames.

From the first, the *Sultana's* paddle wheels had provided life-saving support for great numbers of weak and exhausted swimmers. Many had managed to save themselves, at least temporarily, by grasping one of the wheels or housings. Some rested there briefly, took their bearings or caught a passing plank, and then splashed away. Others clung tenaciously to the precarious havens—in spite of the fire's increasing heat —afraid to stay, but more afraid to let go.

Now, however, it was let go or die. Like broad twin towers, the paddle-wheel housings reached all the way from the water to the promenade, and with the collapse of the upper deck, the towers were left unsupported at the top. Slowly at first, then with great hesitant jerks, they began to lean outward, threatening to topple away from the boat at any moment.

"Sanders, here's a door under the wheel. Let's get it out." Otto Bardon of the 102nd Ohio was holding to the starboard housing with one hand and fishing under the wheel with the other. His friend Fritz Sanders helped, and the two men pulled a glass-paneled door into view.

133

"Let this go," said Bardon. "Here's a whole door."

While Sanders and Bardon pushed away from the wheel with the second door, which was solid wood, several other men set out on the first. Seconds later Bardon looked back and saw the housing fall. If they had remained there one minute longer, they would have been buried in the fire.

At almost the same instant, on the opposite side of the boat, Lieutenant George B. McCord of the 111th Ohio—who had spent the winter at Andersonville—swam away from the larboard housing. Moments after he left the paddle wheel, he saw it make a blazing arc and smash into the river.

The brass mooring rings, which were embedded in the packet's hull every twenty or thirty feet, also offered hope to the floundering. But William H. Norton of the 115th Ohio discovered after leaping from the main deck, that they could also be a deathtrap. As he rose to the surface, several men jumped on top of him, and they all went down together. With his lungs aching, Norton managed to untangle himself and get his head above water. Finding it impossible to swim through the crowd—once he was caught and almost drowned—he instinctively turned back to the boat.

Just as he seized one of the mooring rings, a man locked frantic arms around Norton's chest. "Let go!" Norton yelled. But the man, making no answer, only tightened his grip. Hanging onto the ring with one hand, Norton tried to knock the man loose, knowing that if he let go of the ring, both he and the other man would drown. Yet his arm, twisted and taut, was numbing from the strain. Another man got hold of the ring; still another grasped Norton by the throat; and a vicious struggle began raging at his shoulder. Then the nearby paddle-wheel housing fell, and it seemed to Norton that the whole boat was coming apart. In a fit of desperation, with his last measure of strength, he gouged and wriggled himself free of the man on his back. Kicking away from the boat, he found that the crowd had scattered, and this time he managed to get into the open river.

At about two-forty-five, when the paddle-wheel housings fell, the brisk northerly breeze was still blowing, and the *Sultana* was still drifting stern-first. Because the wind was sweeping from bow to stern the flames had traveled and were still traveling more rapidly in that direction. Now they were licking at the taffrail, driving the last procrastinators off the after section.

As the blaze ate away at the boat's fantail, Nathaniel Foglesong of the 18th Michigan—his friends called him Thaniel—climbed onto the railing. He had lingered because he could not swim, and he intended to prolong his stay until the last possible moment. By standing on tiptoe and stretching one arm and leg, he could just manage to touch the rudder post with his fingers and foot. By leaning far out—so far that he could never get back—he found that he could loop his arm around the rod. And there he stayed until the flames burned his boot. Then jerking his foot off the railing and hugging the rod with both arms, he slid suddenly down onto the shoulders of a man below.

"Get off from me!" the man shouted in alarm.

"In a minute," replied Thaniel.

Nine men were hanging onto the rudder post, each

screaming at those above to get off, and being screamed at in turn by those below. Since Foglesong was on top, he was the only one who kept quiet. But when hot coals began dropping onto his head and shoulders, he realized that his own position was the most dangerous of all.

A large piece of the boiler deck burned off and fell sizzling into the water. Foglesong urged the men below to leave the rudder post and get onto this blackened flotsam which was bobbing nearby.

"My God," protested one, "If we let go of this, we'll drown!"

With the coals showering thicker and faster, Foglesong was at last forced to make the dreaded leap.

"Here goes for ninety days!" he shouted.

Spluttering to the surface he grabbed a convenient ankle. The man who owned it kicked him off, and Foglesong went under for the second time. Fighting for breath, he again seized the same ankle, while with the other hand he caught onto a wire cable which dangled from the blazing stern. Then a short length of three-by-four floated by, and with its help Foglesong dog-paddled his way to the piece of deck. Several others had reached it first, and one of them, a Sergeant Borns, held down a helping hand.

"My God, Thaniel, is that you?"

"Yes, all that's left of me."

On his new sanctuary—it had an area of several hundred square feet—Foglesong stumbled over the burned bodies of a man and two women. He also came across a door, which he dragged to the edge. Sliding the door into the water, he gave it a shove and sent it gliding toward the rudder. With the heat now almost unbearable, the eight holders-on readily abandoned their precarious perch, and aided by the door, all succeeded in reaching the wreckage. It was about three o'clock and they were the last men to leave the stern.

While the flames were being driven aft by the wind, a close-packed congregation had taken refuge on the bow. Here were Simeon Chelf and A. M. Jacobs of Wilson's Lightning Brigade; William Boor, still clutching the spare shirt he had tied up in a rubber blanket; George Robinson, numbed by his fall into the furnaces and the loss of his friend John Corliss; Harvey Ennis, the naval lieutenant who had boarded the *Sultana* at Memphis, with his wife, child and sister-in-law; the newly wedded Hardins—some five hundred persons altogether. For sixty interminable minutes they had endured the terror, resisted the panic and dodged the fire, hoping that some miracle would make it unnecessary for them to plunge into the river.

Through the crowd William Fies of the 64th Ohio caught sight of his friend Robert White, standing with one arm around the jack staff, staring down into the water. Fies knew that White had worked on steamboats before the war, and he pushed to his side, thinking that this was the man who could give him some advice.

"Bob," he asked, "what's to be done?"

White looked up briefly and then turned his gaze back to the water. "Billy," he said, "I guess we'll all be drowned or burned up."

Perhaps this gloomy prophecy was nothing more than simple pessimism, but it may well have been the considered appraisal of an experienced boatman. For White, watching the water and the men struggling beneath the bow, may have noticed something which was not yet apparent to the others: the *Sultana* was swinging around.

Up until the paddle wheels fell, the wind had been splitting at the bow and bearing with equal force against each of the housings, shoving the boat downstream and blowing the blaze toward the stern. Now that the housings were gone, however, the bow had begun falling off to starboard.

At first the movement was slow and almost imperceptible. But it quickly gained in speed and momentum as more and more of the larboard side was presented to the wind. Like a great flaming leaf in a whirlpool, the hull spun about until it had completely reversed itself, with the bow pointing directly downstream and downwind.

Nothing now stood between the flames and the refugees except a thin barrier of wreckage—the remains of the first stairway and portions of the fallen upper decks. Thick billows of smoke, red-flecked with cinders, rolled over the forward section of the boat, and most of the crowd suddenly realized that within moments the blaze would be upon them. Screams pierced the choking air. Men quickly stripped off their clothing. There was a surging, shoving, pushing toward the bow.

Samuel Thrasher and Abraham Rhodes of the 6th Kentucky Cavalry, two more of Wilson's Lightning Raiders, hurriedly knotted a cable line and a heavy chain to a mooring ring and tossed them overboard.

Lieutenant Ennis tried to steady a mule which he had brought to the forward rail, at the same time tightening his grip on the small child in his arms and warning his wife and sister-in-law to stay close, fearing that his family would become separated in the turmoil.

Then with terrifying swiftness, with a great crashing and crackling sound, the fire broke through the barrier and a solid wall of wind-driven flames roared down on the bow. In a broad, unbroken stream, about five hundred people poured into the river, tumbling into the muddy water, piling on top of each other in layers and drowing by the score.

There was no time for a look before the leap. William Boor and Frank Crawford started for the rail at the instant the flames began sweeping the stairway. Crawford jumped first and Boor followed as soon as his friend was out of the way. Yet when he struck the water, Boor heard a hissing noise. In the brief minute that he had delayed on deck his bundle of clothing had caught fire.

Chelf and Jacobs leaped together, still holding onto their precious pieces of wood. Chelf told his companion to "put one end of the board under his breast and hold it there with one hand, paddle with the other hand and to kick with both feet." Jacobs did as he was told and moved away from the boat, while Chelf tucked the small pole under one arm and set out for the Arkansas bank.

Most of the five hundred, however, had nothing to aid them in the water—no planks, no shutters, no barrels—for the bow had long since been stripped of anything that would float. William Fies had gathered a quantity of large splinters from the forward deck and had tied them together with a rope, but he lost even this meager support when he was knocked under water by a man who jumped on top of him—a man whom Fies was certain must have weighed at least two hundred pounds.

One woman was miraculously saved because she was dressed in the height of contemporary fashion—in a fulsome frock which, at first glance, appeared to be a most inappropriate outfit for bathing. With a glorious lack of logic, she had donned all her finery before coming to the bow and when she went overboard, her hoop skirt held enough air to keep her on top of the water.

Unlike the others, Thrasher and Rhodes did not jump at all. They simply slid down the cable and the chain which they had prepared beforehand. Easing gently into the water, they held on for their lives as the struggle surged around them.

The Ennis family was scattered during the leap, just as the lieutenant had feared, and only Mrs. Ennis succeeded in holding onto the rope which her husband had looped about the mule's neck. Her sister went under with a dozen others and never came to the surface. Desperately the terrified Mrs. Ennis clung to the pitching, snorting animal. She saw her husband a few yards away and screamed for help. The lieutenant was struggling to keep himself and the child afloat while dodging the grasp of the drowning; he got the child onto his back and tried to swim toward his wife. As Mrs. Ennis watched, he made a little progress toward her, but soon he and the child sank from sight.

Seth Hardin had lost his bride in the confusion and was swimming savagely through the crowd, screaming her name again and again. He never found her.

Up on the peak of the forecastle stood a Sister of Charity, silhouetted against the fire. Somehow she had avoided being carried overboard, and now she was alone on the blazing *Sultana*. Movingly she pleaded with the thrashing mass, urging the soldiers to stop fighting, stay calm and behave like men. Surprisingly her words seemed to have some effect. Those nearest the boat lost some of their viciousness and ceased some of their clutching and clawing. A few managed to catch onto one of the lines which hung from the bow. When the men shouted to her, imploring her to join them in the water, she refused, knowing that she might become panic-stricken herself and cause the death of another. An instant later she was caught up in the flames.

By three-fifteen—seventy-five minutes after the explosion—there was no living person aboard the *Sultana*.

At this time the *Bostonia No. 2* was still two miles above the Hen and Chickens, and Mr. Keating, the chief pilot, had just noticed that a bright glow was spread across the sky downstream. He examined the phenomenon thoughtfully for a few minutes and concluded, because of its size and brilliance, that it was a forest fire.

Fifteen minutes later he discovered his mistake. As the *Bostonia* rounded a slight bend in the river, the pilothouse window suddenly framed a huge ball of flames, drifting not more than a mile ahead. Instinctively the pilot snatched the bell rope and signaled the engineer, Mr. McGwin, to cut his speed in half.

Aroused by the shouts of Keating and the night watchman, the boat's sleepy officers tumbled out of bed and came running from the texas, buttoning their clothes as they clamored downstairs. Drowsy passengers peeped out of their staterooms to see what the commotion was all about, and were shocked wide-eyed by the blazing specter downstream. Crewmen crowded the lower rails to stare awe-struck at the floating funeral pyre.

By the time Captain Jonathan T. Watson reached the main deck, his boat was plowing into the mile-long string of victims which trailed the derelict like a comet's tail. Mr. Alvord, the chief mate, already had his crewmen scurrying about in search of anything and everything that would float.

Watson gaped at the number of people in the water and even the dim illumination of the distant fire revealed enough bobbing heads to make him cold with horror. Although he could not guess the full extent of the calamity, the captain knew that this was a disaster of staggering magnitude, but for the time being, while he surveyed the situation, he could hardly do more than move ahead at half speed and scatter bales of hay, foot-planks and barrels. He decided not to back water and pick up the men he could see, because he did not know how many others were struggling out of sight in the river ahead; nor did he know how many might be left on the burning wreck.

Of course, the men who were passed by—men who had been praying for the sight of a rescue craft—were in no position to appreciate any such detached and practical view. With leaping hopes they saw the steamboat's bow light appear in the distance; with glad shouts they greeted her approach; and with sick despair they watched her churn away and disappear into the night.

Passing to the right of the *Sultana* and finding her deserted, the *Bostonia* proceeded a short distance farther, then turned in the channel. She plowed back up above the wreck, crowded against the Arkansas timber and dropped her anchor. Immediately the yawl was lowered into the water and willing hands began plucking men and women from drifts and debris— sometimes singly, sometimes in clusters of five or six. Fifteen-year-old Steven Gaston was saved, along with Captain Friesner of the guard company. Also among the first to be brought aboard was the lady in the hoop skirt, who was found floating safely, if uncomfortably, a slighty damp pincushion. One of the *Bostonia's* passengers, a Mr. Deson, went out on a foot-plank and singlehandedly brought back eight persons.

The *Bostonia's* cabin quickly took on the appearance of an emergency hospital—passengers helping Fisher and Lorenz, the steamer's clerks, minister to the patients. After gathering about one hundred survivors, which took just a little over an hour, the boat weighed anchor and raced for Memphis at top speed.

Meanwhile, Robert Hamilton of the 3rd Tennessee Cavalry, in common with most others in the water, was left to his own devices. Despite the fact that Hamilton had a plank and had been laboring to reach the bank since shortly after the explosion, he had found it impossible to escape the current. He and the *Sultana* had drifted close together, and soon after the *Bostonia* left him behind he noticed that several men were climbing back onto the blackened bow.

The men he saw were Kentucky troopers Thrasher and Rhodes and a few more who had escaped the heat by submerging themselves in the water, and had thus managed to hold onto their lines and chains until the fire subsided. With the boat burned almost to the water's edge, two or three of the soldiers—those not weighed down by wet clothing—had pulled themselves up hand over hand. Now they were drawing up others who had gone into the river fully clothed.

As the smoldering hull followed the current downstream, the little party on board continued their angling, dropping their lines over the bow and trolling for humans instead of fish. Hamilton was flopped up on deck, as were Adam Leake and Thomas Pangle, also of the 3rd Tennessee Cavalry, Joshua S. Patterson of the 104th Ohio and W. T. Shummard of the 7th Ohio.

By five o'clock in the morning, the *Sultana,* or what was left of her, had drifted from two to three miles below the point of explosion. In the gray light of dawn, the hull bumped against a grove of saplings which grew in front of the Fogleman plantation, near the Mound City landing. Ordinarily these trees were rooted on the Arkansas shore, on a slight rise of ground. But the flood had washed beyond them, leaving only their topmost branches above water.

W. A. Fast, who had lost his door and his memory, finally regained consciousness on the northern edge of this overflowed timber, not far from the wreck. At sunrise he found himself clinging to what appeared to be a clump of bushes. When he stretched down as far as he could, however, he could not touch bottom. Puzzled, Fast could see forty or fifty acres covered with the same kind of eerie growth—small bushes sprouting from the muddy surface of the river. Then he realized that the leafy sprouts were not bushes at all, but the tips of tall, young willow and cottonwood trees.

A quarter mile downriver, Fast saw the hull of the *Sultana,* still billowing flame and smoke, slowly turning in an eddy. Splashing along from treetop to treetop, he made his way to the wreck and caught one of the lines which hung from the bow. Already exhausted by his ordeal in the water, he began a long, trying struggle to climb aboard.

After nearly an hour of slipping and scuffling, Fast finally pulled himself over the gunwale. While he caught his breath, sprawled on a pile of cast-off clothing and blankets, he counted the men aboard—twenty-three besides himself, five or six of them badly scalded or maimed. The hull, covered with two or three feet of coal, wood and other debris, was alive with fire. Only the bow, for twenty feet or so, offered a safe footing. Facing aft, all of the able-bodied beat at the slowly advancing flames with water-soaked jackets and shirts.

Soon after getting aboard, Fast noticed a man floating downstream on a piece of siding and, as he drew near, recognized Sergeant Owens of Sandusky, Ohio, a friend from Castle Morgan. Fast called to the sergeant and asked him to help tie the hull to a tree.

Picking up one end of a small line, Fast knotted it to the hawser and threw the other end over the side. Owens caught the small line, paddled over to a fallen oak, hauled out the hawser and lashed it tightly to a limb. Then Fast helped Owens aboard, and together they pulled another twelve men out of the water.

Even in her death throes, the *Sultana* continued to kill. Under the guard, near midships on the starboard side, a youngster was still clinging to one of the brass mooring rings. Above him the rail was ablaze, and fire extended on both sides of him for a distance of twenty feet. With the flames inching closer, the boy pleaded for help. His mother in Indiana was well off, he shouted, and if his comrades on the bow would save him, she would give them everything she owned. Fast and the others had one long pole, the only wood available, and this was thrown down to the boy. Being unable to swim, however, he failed to catch it. Next the men tried to float lines along the side of the boat, but each was burned off by the fire. As his lungs became filled with hot air and smoke, the boy's voice grew hoarse and weak, and he talked more and more of his home and mother in Indiana. At last, with the flames closing in, his fingers relaxed; quietly he sank into the river.

From their vantage point at Mound City, John Fogleman and his neighbors watched the ruined steamer drift into the timber, and though she was three-quarters of a mile away, they could make out the men on her bow. It was obvious, even at this distance, that the tiny figures were fighting a losing battle against the fire and that the end was only a matter of time. Agonizingly the minutes dragged into an hour as the anxious little group on the Arkansas shore looked on helplessly. At long last the first rescue boats from Memphis arrived, but none came close, and the men on the wreck went unnoticed.

When inaction could neither be endured nor excused any longer, Fogleman suggested building a raft —a proposal enthusiastically adopted at once. Rope and tools were hurriedly collected, and in the course of another hour, two twelve-foot logs were hewed square and lashed together. With much excited puffing and shouted advice, the crude raft was dragged down the muddy bank and into the river. The plantation owner himself crawled aboard and set out for the still-blazing hull, energetically using a homemade paddle.

It was about eight o'clock, as Fast remembered it, when he and his thirty-six companions saw Fogleman put off from the Arkansas shore. By this time the flames had reduced the sanctuary on the bow to less than fifteen feet, and the sweating soldiers eagerly followed their rescuer's progress. About one hundred feet from the wreck, Fogleman stopped for a parley. He could carry no more than six men at one time, he shouted, and he was afraid that if he came any closer all of the men would jump overboard at once. Fast and another soldier—Fast called him Indiana—stepped to the rail and declared in the most solemn manner that they would stay on the hull themselves and that they would allow no more than six others to get onto the raft.

Accepting this assurance, Fogleman paddled under the bow. Immediately, six men swarmed down the lines, into the water and onto the logs. Speed was imperative, because of the fire, and after taking his passengers halfway to shore, the plantation owner put them into the trees. Hurrying back to the hull he ferried away a second load, and then a third, following the same procedure. When he returned for the fourth time, however, he said that it was taking the weary, wasted parolees too long to climb the trees and that he would have to carry the remainder to the bank.

As Fogleman left with the fourth group, the position of the thirteen men still aboard the wreck suddenly became desperate. Although the after deck was saturated with water, it at last burned through at a point near the rudder. The flames then swept down the length of the cargo hold and up through the hatch near the prow. With fire on both sides and under their feet, the soldiers dipped up water with canteen cups, poured it over their heads and waited frantically for the raft's return.

Realizing that the next trip might be the last, Fast, Indiana and the other able-bodied men held a hurried conference. Should they take to the raft and leave the scalded and maimed behind? The injured, overhearing the debate, begged their comrades not to abandon them. When Fogleman arrived, Fast and the others, exchanging glances of silent agreement, lowered the helpless onto the raft. Then someone said, "Seven will have to go this load or the next." Shouting, "Seven go this load," Fast slid down a cable, straddled the logs and with hands and feet helped pull for the shore.

Quickly clearing the raft with the help of his neighbors, Fogleman pounded his way back to the wreck.

With frenzied agility the last half-dozen soldiers scrambled over the side and dropped onto the logs, almost overcome with heat and smoke. Before the raft had traveled a hundred feet toward the bank, the men heard a noise and turned their heads just in time to see the hull go down.

With a long, loud gasping sound the *Sultana* settled to the bottom and disappeared, leaving only the jack staff above water. Sighing at the sudden quenching of the fire, she slipped from sight, while a thick pillar of smoke rolled skyward in a wraithlike memorial above the churning water of her burial place.

VI

Acres of
Agony

At three-thirty, an hour and a half after the *Sultana*
explosion, the Memphis wharf still dozed in unsuspecting tranquillity. Along the three miles of planking
there was no movement except the gentle rocking of
a dozen moored packets, naval gunboats and other
vessels; no sound except the scraping of mossy timbers, the creaking of hempen lines and the whispering
rush of the flood-swollen Mississippi. Behind and
above the landing, the city of thirty thousand slept.
No traffic stirred on the broad avenue which followed
the crest of the bluff, nor on the narrower intersecting
streets which slanted down to the river.

Near the center of the landing lay the wharf boat, a
small, nondescript craft—a floating office from which
the business of the port was conducted. Inside the

lantern-lit cabin, with the door ajar, two men sat nodding in straight chairs, beside a potbellied stove. Hearing a noise, the two men roused, looked at each other quizzically and stepped out on deck. Then they heard it again—a cry for help coming from the river. While one man held the lantern high, the other jumped into a skiff and rowed out into the stream. Only a few yards away, in the dim wash of the kerosene light, he found a thin, half-naked boy, Wesley Lee of the 102nd Ohio, clinging to a pair of boards.

Lee had wasted no time in leaving the *Sultana* after her boilers burst. Pausing only to remove his outer clothing, he had ripped two pine planks from the lower stairway and jumped overboard on the starboard side. The firelight illuminated the trees on the Tennessee bank and he swam toward this haven. When an hour of exhausting labor brought him no nearer to his goal, Wesley realized that the current was running against him and that his efforts were only accelerating his movement downstream. But he decided not to change his course, reasoning that farther along the current might shift in his favor.

Because he had continued to struggle toward the Tennessee side, Wesley Lee became the first man to arrive at Memphis with word of the disaster. After Lee was helped aboard the wharf boat, he told his rescuers about the *Sultana*. One of the men, a telegrapher, rushed to his key and tapped out the news.

Afterward it would be said that the report was first given by the *General Boynton*, a military courier boat which had started upstream from Memphis a short time earlier and had turned back as soon as she

151

discovered that the river was full of struggling people. According to Lee, however, the *Boynton* arrived several minutes behind him and claimed the credit with his permission. While Lee was warming at the stove on the wharf boat, the *Boynton* laid alongside and put off several parolees she had just picked up. Since it was customary at Memphis and other river cities to pay a bounty to the first boat bringing news of a disaster, the telegraph operator asked Lee if he wanted to be mentioned as the person who had given the information. It would do Lee no good, but the crew of the *Boynton* would get paid for it. Wesley agreed and the *General Boynton* was given the credit.

During the ninety minutes that had elapsed between the explosion and Lee's arrival at the wharf boat, twelve to fifteen hundred *Sultana* survivors—those who had somehow managed to escape the concussion, the steam, the falling wreckage, the fire and the stampede—had become scattered across five thousand acres of treacherous Mississippi River. Faced with the staggering task of searching them out before they died, the authorities at Memphis moved quickly. To Captain Curtis, master of river transportation, went the telegraph operator's message. At once the word was passed to Captain Senior of the river guard, with instructions to notify the commander of every vessel at the wharf. Curtis also ordered three steamers—the *Jenny Lind,* the military picket boat *Pocahontas* and a ferry named *Rosadella*—to fire up immediately and to proceed upstream the moment pressure could be raised.

By four o'clock—a half hour after Lee was pulled

out of the water and still a half hour before the *Bostonia* would leave the disaster scene on her race for Memphis—the river in front of the city was clogged with swimmers. Desperate and near drowning, many of them badly scalded and injured, they had been afloat for as much as two hours. Numbed by exposure, holding onto their frail pieces of debris with ebbing strength, they saw the city lights. Scared and screaming, their voices ripped out of the black night. From steamers along the river front came an answer of clanging bells and scurrying feet. Buckets of pitch pine and tar were dragged onto the decks and set ablaze, while crewmen clamored into lifeboats and set their oarlocks squealing.

Small craft from the U.S. Iron-Clad *Essex*, the U.S.S. *Grosbeak* and the U.S.S. *Tyler* were engaged in the rescue work, as were a dozen or more steamboat yawls and river-front skiffs. A yawl from the *Marble City* picked up seventeen men. And while the *Pocahontas* was building steam, the pilot and engineer went out in a yawl and found five or six.

Ensign James H. Berry, executive officer of the *Essex*, was awakened by quartermaster Thomas C. Love, who excitedly told him that the *Sultana* had blown up and was burning a short distance up the river. Since the captain, Lieutenant John C. Parker, was spending the night ashore, Berry was in charge of the man-of-war, and he promptly ordered all small boats to be manned and launched.

The young ensign himself took command of the larger cutter, the first boat to be lowered into the water. Close behind him came the smaller cutter, with Love at the helm. And the captain's coxswain, John Thompson, took the tiller of the gig. As soon as these three boats were safely out of sight, the six messenger boys of the *Essex,* with questionable authority but laudable motives, set out in the dinghy or market boat.

Most of the shrieks and groans seemed to be coming from the Arkansas side of the river, and Berry's two-man crew rowed in that direction. At length they were able to distinguish the voices of six men shouting together, and they steered toward the chorus. Visibility was less than twenty feet, and the oarsmen were guided by sound alone until they were almost on top of the survivors.

P. L. Horn, who had been "lost in the air" by the explosion, was the first man to be pulled into the cutter. He had clung to the twenty-foot section of boiler-deck guard rail along with five companions—two others having slipped off and drowned on the way downstream.

As he tumbled headfirst into the rescue boat, Horn heard a gasp from one of the men left behind in the water, "For God's sake, help me in."

Recognizing the voice of Joseph McKelvy, his bunkmate, Horn grasped the upraised hand and asked, "Are you hurt?"

"Yes," replied McKelvy, "scalded from head to foot."

Berry helped get McKelvy aboard and then took off his coat and put it around the injured man to cover his blistering flesh. After the other four were hauled to safety, the sailors headed upstream with their shivering passengers. By this time the cutter had drifted three miles below the city, opposite Fort Pickering.

As the boat headed crosscurrent toward the Tennessee bank, one of the fort's Negro pickets raised his rifle and sent a shot thudding into the water nearby. The cutter hove to and pulled in closer to shore. "Why did you shoot at me?" yelled Berry.

"I obeyed my orders," replied the sentry.

The ensign hurriedly explained what had happened and told the soldier that he was picking up drowning men. The sentry made no reply, and the cutter proceeded to the wharf, where the six survivors, transferred to the packet *Marble City,* found other victims of the disaster. Crewmen spread a pallet for McKelvy on the main deck, gently removed his clothing and sprinkled his body with flour—the boatman's standard first-aid remedy for scalds and burns. An equally time-honored but considerably less effective treatment was visited on an unconscious man who appeared to be gorged with water. For some time he was vigorously rolled across a barrel, in spite of which (or because of which) he died.

Berry and his crew returned to the middle of the river and fell in with the gig, near a pile of drift which was covered with men. Soon a steamboat yawl came out to help in gathering up the survivors, who were so stiff and benumbed that they had to be handled like dead men. Before half of them had been pulled out of the water, another shot, fired by the Fort Pickering sentry, came whistling overhead. Although the boats made a large target, Berry and the others refused to leave the drift until all of the men had been rescued.

Later, near sunrise, Berry finally went to the fort, upbraided the confused sentry and had a loud argument with Lieutenant D. P. Yates, the fort's field officer of the day, who came down to investigate.

"Why was I fired at?" demanded Berry.

"We are ordered to fire a warning shot at all skiffs," snapped Yates.

"These boats are not skiffs; they are a man-of-war's gig and cutter."

"Our sentinels are instructed to bring to all small boats passing up or down the river, by discharging their pieces."

"For the sake of humanity, why can't you execute your orders with some discretion in a time like this?"

"I have as much humanity as anyone!"

"That"—pointing to three skiffs lying hauled up on the bank—"doesn't look much like humanity!"

Berry returned to the river in high dudgeon, and the next day he made a formal report of the incident, charging that the officers and men at Fort Pickering had callously refused to offer any assistance to the *Sultana* survivors.

In fact, when they finally became aware of what was happening, the officers of the fort and the thirty or forty soldiers of the 3rd U. S. Colored Artillery who were garrisoned there, did all that they could. The three skiffs joined the rescue flotilla, and more than one hundred survivors were landed at the fort. Fires were built to dry them out, and they were given whiskey, coffee, meat and bread. Some twenty-five of the most seriously injured were placed in the post hospital until ambulances arrived from Memphis; several of the Negro patients gave up their beds to those who had greater need of them.

The men who had been blown overboard by the explosion were among the first to reach Memphis and many of these—like Horn and his comrades—were rescued by boats from the *Essex*. Early on the scene and working below the city, Berry and his sailors intercepted Jotham W. Maes and the nine other men who had ridden into the river on a piece of the boiler deck. Maes and his companions had found that the wreckage was just large enough to support them all, so long as they remained neck-deep in the water and kept themselves evenly distributed around the edge.

Stewart Oxley of the 51st Ohio and another man were pried loose from a board and lifted into the gig, three miles below Memphis. As they were put onto the deck of the *Essex*, the ironclad's surgeon poured a glass of whiskey down each one, while the crewmen cut down their hammocks to make pallets for the survivors and helped to remove their wet clothing. Oxley had caught onto the board just after being blown into the river. Minutes later he had lapsed into unconsciousness, and he remembered nothing of his ten-mile trip down the river.

Samuel H. Raudebaugh of the 65th Ohio, who was picked up two miles below the city by the quartermaster's cutter, had also awakened in the water. Seeing the *Sultana*'s icebox floating nearby, he had tried to get onto it, but a swarm of other men with the same idea had frightened him away. Some distance downstream he had found the piece of wreckage which brought him to Memphis—a complete four-foot section of a stairway banister.

Ira B. Horner, another of those hurled off the boiler

deck and saved by crewmen of the *Essex,* admitted
that he was "not very well versed in the art of swimming." When he landed in the water, a small timber
landed beside him, and with this support he knew that
he could stay afloat. Most of the time he worried about
something entirely different: the *Sultana*'s mascot,
the seven-and-a-half foot alligator that he feared
might be free in the water. As he worried his way
downstream, he heard someone shout, "Horner, is
that you?"

"Yes, what are you floating on?"

"A piece of the hurricane deck."

"Is it big enough for me, too?"

"Yes, Horner, come along."

Leaving his timber, Horner swam toward the voice
and soon found a member of his company and two
other men holding onto a four-by-six-foot piece of
wreckage. Although the float was hardly large enough
for four, Horner's timber was gone and he had to remain. For more than an hour the little party floated
quietly along. Then, a mile above Memphis, they were
suddenly fired upon by one of the city guards. A few
minutes later, seeing the wharf lights, Horner shouted
for help with all his strength. One of the boats from
the *Essex* found the men, picked them up and rowed
them back to the ironclad, where they were given
whiskey, hardtack and dried beef. More than sixty
men were rescued by the crew of the *Essex* and all
probably agreed with Horner who said, "I felt like if I
had all the world I would give it to those boatmen."

Not all were so lucky. Between the time of Wesley
Lee's arrival and the moment of dawn more than an

hour later, hundreds of survivors bobbed along the stretch of river in front of the Memphis bluffs. They could not be seen, only heard. Inevitably, many were missed and were forced to continue their harrowing journey until they lodged somewhere on the shore below or were drowned.

John Kochenderfer clung to a candlebox until he had traveled fifteen miles. Hours after the explosion, he and four others were found, near death, on the bank of President's Island.

Joseph Bringman saw the buildings along the Memphis water front as he floated past on the Arkansas side, and he heard the shouts of rescuers and the clang of steamer bells. But although he yelled at the top of his lungs, he was not noticed. "I was so chilled that I was powerless," he wrote, "and a kind of drowsiness came over me. I felt that I was going to sleep, and I seemed as comfortable as if in a downy bed. I soon dropped to sleep, or to unconsciousness, with the music of the bells of the steamers ringing in my ears." It was late in the day before he was picked up, far beyond the city, limp and senseless, with a fractured arm, three broken ribs, a scalded face and numberless cuts and bruises.

Before sunrise, the three steamers ordered out by Captain Curtis—the *Jenny Lind,* the *Pocahontas* and the *Rosadella*—were on their way from Memphis to the scene of the disaster. They left only a few minutes apart, and all met the *Bostonia* as she hurried downstream with her cargo of survivors.

Meanwhile, in the river's cold, black water, the vicious fight for survival continued, among men who had learned their lessons in the hard schools of Andersonville and Cahaba.

J. W. Rush made his way downstream for a half hour with the aid of a small plank, until he at last bumped against a door, which offered safer support in his struggle toward the Arkansas timber. "All this time," he remembered, "I could hear people calling and praying for help, while others who were reasonably secure upon stage planks, bales of hay and so forth were using their old prison slang—'lie down and keep cool,' 'hot skillet,' 'fresh fish,' 'keep your hands on your pocketbook,' and 'swim or die.' " In the water, as on the *Sultana*, it was every man for himself.

After losing his bundle of splinters in the leap from the bow, William Fies somehow managed to get clear of the crowd, although he was a poor swimmer and had a badly dislocated shoulder. "When I was just about exhausted and thought my time had come," he wrote, "I came to a fellow with a nice large board. He was the only occupant, but I saw at once that he was very much excited and was not making any headway."

Fies threw his disabled left arm over the board.

"For God's sake let go," the man cried, "I'm drowning!"

"You fool," said Fies, "this board's large enough to save both of us and several more, if managed right."

But the man was not reassured. Trying fantically to shake Fies loose, he spun the plank over and over, tumbling under water with almost every revolution. Fies kept calm, occasionally putting his hands on the board to keep himself afloat. At length the man, exhausted by his own frenzied exertions, sank beneath the water. As soon as Fies had full possession of the plank, he quickly kicked his way downstream, afraid that another crazed survivor might want to take passage with him. For a long hour he rode the tide, keeping a watchful eye on his fellow travelers. At last he sighted a line of treetops—the overflowed shore of Hen Island—and a few minutes later he caught onto the limbs of a small cottonwood. Nearly helpless, he failed in his first attempt to climb the sapling, slipping back into the water and almost drowning. But on the second try he succeeded in perching himself on a branch.

On his way to the Arkansas timber, M. C. White had a similar encounter with a berserker, except that he wound up the loser. Having jumped overboard just after helping Big Kentuck in his unsuccessful effort to free one of the trapped men, White managed to get through the crowd near the boat and found a sizable plank. Before he had traveled far, however, another soldier seized the float and tried to take it away from him. White reasoned and pleaded, but at every word the man lunged toward him, grabbing and shouting. Afraid that the man would catch hold of his clothes, White let go and swam away. Unable to see which way to go, he floated passively downstream. At dawn, as he was rounding a bend in the river near Memphis, the current washed him toward the west shore, and he managed to reach the treetops.

Another of the Arkansas tree-hangers, George Young, had overcome two threats—the deadly clutch of drowning men and the unexpectedly dangerous drag of his government-issue drawers. Twice, as he swam away from the *Sultana,* Young was seized and pulled under water. Fighting his way out of the crowd, near exhaustion, he decided to take off his sodden, cumbersome drawers. Loosing them at the waist, he let them drop, but he had forgotten that the long legs were fastened at the bottom by ankle strings. The dangling drawers, binding his feet together, made it almost impossible to swim. Only after a long and tiring struggle did he succeed in pulling them back up.

Young soon became aware of an aching in his left hand. Holding it up to the light of the burning boat, he discovered that his wrist, thumb and two fingers were badly blistered and swollen. Keeping the hand beneath the water to relieve the pain, he rode the current downstream, making a collection of flotsam as he moved along—a pair of trousers, a small piece of roofing, half of a cork life preserver and a cracker box. Later, after an hour or so alone, he heard a "hello" in the dark and held a long-distance conversation with a man who said he was riding a log. Although the man refused, according to Young, "in words more forcible than refined," to share his float, the two formed a partnership to find the shore. Seeing a treetop against the sky, Young paddled toward it, with the help of his debris, and caught onto a limb. As he drew himself out of the water, Young shouted to the man with the log, and he also made his way into the timber.

Many of the swimmers who had witnessed the carnival of death at the *Sultana*'s bow and stern were so terrified that they would allow no one to come near them. Truman Smith, the young Michigan cavalryman, heard a man coughing and swam toward him, but the man kept swimming away. "I called to him," wrote Smith, "and asked what regiment he belonged to. He asked what I wanted to know for. I told him I would write to his people in case he drowned and I should get out. He said I must not come any closer, and we made a bargain that if one should die and the other get ashore the survivor would write the parents and let them know."

Smith and his unseen companion swam near each other until just before sunrise. As they approached the Tennessee bank above Memphis, a sentry from the city's garrison shouted, "Halt!" Smith told him they could not halt, they were in the water. When the two reached the bank, the suspicious picket leveled his rifle and told them to get out of the river. But the panting men could obey this second command no better than the first, and the sentry at last came down to the water's edge and helped them ashore.

In the alligator box, William Lugenbeal tried to make the Arkansas timber as long as it was lighted by the burning steamer. After the fire died down, however, he lost all sense of direction. Still fearful that his craft would be seized and swamped, he drifted quietly through the lonely darkness, making no sound. At one point a man swam by and shouted, "Here goes your old tugboat." But Lugenbeal said nothing, since he "had tug enough" of his own. The tight-lipped Lugenbeal was eventually picked up by a boat from the *Essex*.

When men met in the water on this dark and terrible night, the meeting was often fatal. Yet the most deadly conflict was not between man and man, but rather between man and the Old Man. The paroled prisoners were weak—pitifully weak—and the Father of Waters was wily and strong. His traps included vines and whirlpools; his allies were buffalo gnats and mosquitoes; and his tricks could cloud the mind, transforming exposure into delirium and exhaustion into death.

Chester Berry, whose skull had been fractured as he slept on the main deck, began swimming toward a wall of willows which appeared to be no more than a half mile away. Minute after minute he lashed at the water, with his board under one arm, panting for breath and aching in every muscle. Yet he seemed to be caught on a treadmill, and no matter how hard he worked, the willows remained at the same distance, like a tantalizing, unreachable mirage. When he stopped to rest, Berry glanced over his shoulder, and beyond the burning *Sultana* he saw the bow lights of a boat—the *General Boynton*. When he looked back at the willows, he found that they were farther away than ever, and he realized that he had been trying to swim upstream. Already exhausted, he turned back and made for the *Boynton*. But before he was well past the blazing wreck, which he kept a safe distance on his left, the lights of the courier boat disappeared.

Overcome by an irresistible drowsiness, Berry dropped off to sleep, dreamed vividly of his home in Michigan and did not awaken until long after sunrise. Slowly regaining consciousness, he found himself standing on a large snag in the river, his feet resting on a prong a foot below water. Out of his senses, he imagined that some terrible danger threatened him, but that if he could only get his board onto an upper prong of the snag, two feet above water, he would be safe. Struggling with the plank for several minutes, he finally realized that putting it onto the prong would do no good and he began to cry with the pain of his fractured skull.

As his thoughts became clearer, Berry saw that he was less than a hundred feet from the Arkansas timber. Shoving his plank into the water, he splashed over to the treetops and pulled himself onto the limb of a cottonwood. Instantly surrounded by a swarm of mosquitos and buffalo gnats, he seated himself firmly on the limb, ripped two leafy branches from the sapling and frantically tried to whip the insects off his body. In spite of his efforts, his face, neck and chest were soon solid blotches of red.

As the *General Boynton* approached, having passed by many, Captain Elliott and his uninvited passenger were working their way downstream on the mattress which Elliott had thrown from the boiler deck. From a distance of nearly three-quarters of a mile, they watched the little steamer heave to, heard her whistle and then saw her turn back for Memphis. Held prisoner by the current, the two men floated three miles before striking a small stationary drift on the Arkansas shore. Crawling onto a cypress, Elliott found that his legs were so chilled he could hardly move them. In his pocket he had three packets of quinine, given to him by a Sister of Charity, and he took all three doses at once. After a few minutes of vigorous rubbing he was able to stand and walk. His companion, meanwhile, was helpless and unable to get onto the drift. Breaking off a limber switch and holding the mattress in close, Elliott struck the man again and again. Each time the switch fell, the man groaned and begged and rubbed his smarting skin. Roused by the whipping, he was soon able, with the captain's help, to climb onto the cypress. Together the two men pulled a young woman and two other soldiers out of the water, but all three died of exposure within minutes.

While the *Boynton,* quickly reversing directions, was noticed by only a few score of the swimmers, the downward-bound *Bostonia* was seen by hundreds. Simeon Chelf of the 6th Kentucky Cavalry, with the pole he had received in unequal trade from A. M. Jacobs, was paddling toward the Arkansas shore when the *Bostonia* churned between him and the bank, tossing off bales of hay. As the packet's wake washed back toward mid-river, Chelf was strangled by the muddy water slapping him in the face, but, with a bit of experimenting, he learned to dive through one wave and ride the next.

When he was within four hundred yards of the bank, and after the water had calmed somewhat, another young soldier overtook Chelf and said, "Hi, pard, haven't you got something I could rest my hand on until we get to the bushes?"

"Do you have on any clothes?" asked Chelf.

"Yes, I've got my shirt on."

"Well, take it off and you can swim better."

Treading water, the soldier removed his shirt, and Chelf shoved his pole to the boy. One on each end, the two kicked together and soon landed among the scrubs and saplings.

Looking for a way out of the water, Chelf sloshed around through the brush for more than an hour, shouting, "Has anybody found land?" Finally a voice answered, "Here's a good dry log you can get on." Chelf and his invisible friend yelled back and forth until Chelf found the log. Helped out of the water, with the blood pounding into his head, Chelf suddenly became blind. By rubbing and hitting himself on the chest, he quickened the circulation through his body and shook off the blindness. Then he jumped up and down until he began to sweat. At dawn, when the mosquitos descended in swarms, both men spent their time slapping and scratching.

Two others who saw the *Bostonia* pass were Otto Bardon and Fritz Sanders. As they pushed away from the *Sultana's* paddle wheel with their door, Bardon said, "Let's go to the right, it's nearer to shore."

"No," said Sanders, "there's a boat. Let's paddle for it."

So for a few minutes they pursued the *Bostonia*, but she steamed out of sight before they had reached the center of the river.

Turning back toward the Arkansas side, they passed three men on a large trunk who were finding it difficult to steer their heavy and unwieldy buoy. One of the men grasped the door and asked Bardon and Sanders to guide them into the timber. But this added burden proved too much, and the door sank. "Boys," said Bardon, "if you don't keep your weight off of the door, then you'll have to steer the trunk yourselves." He added emphasis to this warning by giving the trunk a vicious kick, and as the three men relaxed their grip, the door bobbed back to the surface.

With the help of the current, all of the men reached the timber on Hen Island. Here they separated, fanning out through the treetops, each making his own search for a large limb or drift. Bardon, too weak to climb, wrapped his arms around the trunk of a cottonwood and held on, neck deep in the water, praying aloud and using first one hand and then the other to brush the mosquitoes off his face.

L. W. McCrory, with his iron-bound pocketbook still in his hand, was one of the few *Sultana* survivors who made his way into the timber without the help of box, board, barrel or float of any kind. For a long time he swam downstream, his pocketbook in one hand and his valise in the other. Beside him was John Cornwell, another member of the 100th Ohio, who also had nothing to aid him in the water. Cornwell was easily discouraged and after a time, he shouted that he could not swim any longer. Several times McCrory cheered him up, saying he knew Cornwell could hold out until they reached the shore, but after going another two or three miles, Cornwell cried out that it was no use and immediately sank. "This startled me a little," admitted McCrory and so he dropped his valise with its suit of citizen's clothes, but held onto the pocketbook and its hundred dollars. Seized with cramps in his arms, he alternately swam and floated until he struck a log on the Arkansas side, about two miles above Memphis.

While waiting for a boat to find him, McCrory

watched a man pulled out of the water by two other soldiers—there wasn't a particle of skin on his entire body because of the scalding he had received on the *Sultana*. McCrory watched while the rescuers did their best to keep the buffalo gnats off this agonized victim of live steam.

George Robinson, who had already proved himself a master at escape, reached safety with the help of a dead mule. As he swam away from the *Sultana's* bow, Robinson "kept up good courage" and felt sure that he could reach the shore. But after two hours in the current-strong Mississippi, he had lost most of the feeling in his legs and nearly all his confidence. Just as he was about to sink, he saw a dark object in the water and made for it. It was a dead mule. Robinson climbed on and discovered that the mule not only continued to float, but was still warm. Four hours after the explosion, he was taken off this strange raft by one of the boats from Fort Pickering.

Hiram Allison of the 9th Indiana Cavalry had been in the water for more than an hour when he met two men holding the ends of a horse trough and praying with their eyes tight shut. Allison grabbed the center of the trough and spoke to them, but neither man paused in his prayers, and Allison did not try to interrupt again. He was so busy with his own efforts to stay awake and afloat that he did not notice when the praying voices became still and it was not until daylight that he realized the men were gone. Praying now himself, Allison managed to hold on to the trough until he reached a drift log on the Arkansas shore.

At about the same time that the first rescue boats

started upstream from Memphis, a skiff and a dugout canoe began picking up survivors from the Arkansas treetops and from the Mound City island of timber. In the skiff were William Boardman and R. K. Hill, operators of the woodyard located a short distance north of Mound City; and in the canoe was Frank Barkton, a Confederate lieutenant who had been camping close by.

Poling through the brush, Barkton found Ben Davis, whose canteen had been wrenched out of his hand by the explosion, and John Andorf, huddled on a drift log. After hurrying them to the woodyard, Barkton discovered an unconscious man clinging half-frozen to a tree limb and had to cut the limb to get him down. He pushed desperately toward a soldier on a willow, only to see him relax his hold and slip beneath the water when the canoe was less than a length away.

And that is the way it was, up and down the river, both in the dark hours before sunrise and in the light of morning. The difference between life and death could be measured. It was a matter of yards, feet, inches. It was the length of a reaching arm that was long enough, or a little too short. Sometimes the difference could also be reckoned in time. It was a matter of hours, minutes, seconds. It was the help that came in time, or a little too late.

In the case of Charlie King the difference was shorter than an inch and less than a second. Lieutenant Swain pushed the plank and the frightened soldier who rode it until his breath was coming in painful gasps. King's legs and arms were wrapped around the board in silent terror, and he made no sound even in

response to Swain's words of encouragement. At last
the board bumped against a tangle of drift, and both
men clawed and scrambled onto the pile. Suddenly
King slipped and tumbled into the water. Swain made
a grab and his finger tips brushed against the youngster's upraised hand just before it vanished into the
muddy flood. Later, Swain was rescued by Barkton—
the lieutenant in gray saving the lieutenant in blue.

As Barkton was working his way along the northern
edge of the Mound City timber, he heard the voice of
George Young, the Ohioan with the worrisome drawers
and the scalded hand, shouting out of the night.

"Where are you?" yelled Barkton.

"In a tree right here, only a little way from you!"

"Well, cling to the limb and come toward me, and
you can touch ground with your feet."

Following instructions, Young and his companion
waded out to the canoe, and Barkton poled them
through the shallow water to the woodyard—a small
clearing stacked with cords of pine and fronted by a
shanty cabin. A porchlike platform of logs had been
built onto the cabin to accommodate refueling steamers. On this platform and peering through a window,
Young could see that the shanty's single room was already crowded with survivors. So for several minutes
he and the other man walked the platform, trying to
warm themselves by swinging their arms and stamp-
ing their feet. Soon, however, the night wind drove
them inside. Two women, scantily dressed and soaking wet, were sitting on a rail bench beside the fire-
place; two soldiers, badly scalded and burned, lay
writhing on a bed; and two other soldiers, injured and

exhausted, were sprawled on the floor. Hoping to find some cloth to cover his scalded hand, Young searched the corners of the cabin and discovered a barrel of flour. Politely he asked if he might use some of it for his burns. No one admitted owning the flour, but the women urged Young to take what he needed. Dipping lightly into the barrel, he spread the soothing powder over his smarting, aching fingers and wrist.

Shortly after sunup, Boardman and Hill, the wood-yard owners and presumably the owners of Young's flour returned to their cabin, bringing with them Albert King and the woman whom King had helped away from the stern of the *Sultana*.

For more than an hour King and the woman had floated downstream on their plank, until they struck the timber in front of Mound City. During all of this time the woman had spoken little, except that occasionally she would ask, "For God's sake, tell me, do you think we'll be saved?" And to this question King had made no reply, because he was afraid that the answer was no.

"All at once," King wrote, "my feet came in contact with brush. This encouraged me, and I worked fast, fearing that if it was an island under water we might accidentally pass it. I now saw that we were among small trees and brush, but my feet would not reach bottom. The current was sweeping over this island and it carried us down. Fortunately we were now within reach of a drift lodged against saplings. I soon discovered a log among the drift, which I mounted. It sank partly, and I had no trouble in seating my companion. I held her with one hand, grasping the little tree next to me with the other. Our weight upon the log brought it down and we were in the water to our shoulders. In a few minutes we became so chilled that we could scarcely speak. Soon it was daylight, and no one in sight who might rescue us from our dangerous position."

Later Boardman and Hill came near. They almost passed King and his companion, but someone behind them called to the boat to run in for a man and woman in the drift. Boardman and Hill obeyed, and in a few minutes King and the woman were lying in the bottom of the boat. At the cabin, King found George Hill of his company, who spoke to the woman, and while they were talking, she drew a ring from her finger and handed it to King, saying it was all she had to offer him as a token of reward.

While one of the woodyard men remained at the cabin to care for the survivors, the other rowed back to look for more. On the eastern fringe of the Mound City timber, he found Daniel McLeod, the Shiloh pensioner, groaning with the pain of his two broken ankles, and Ogilvie Hamblin, holding to a treetop with his one arm and screaming for help.

The woodman got both McLeod and Hamblin into the boat and had started back when he saw a little girl fighting to keep her head above water. The child, about seven years old, wore a life preserver which had slipped low on her waist, throwing her head downward. All three men tried frantically to reach the youngster—the oarsman straining to row closer, McLeod dragging himself half over the gunwale, and Hamblin tottering precariously as he stretched his only arm. In their frenzy of effort the trio almost upset the boat; as each man struggled to regain his balance, the tiny feet with their miniature high-heeled gaiters disappeared.

McLeod and Hamblin were landed at the woodyard, sopping wet and trembling like leaves. But while McLeod was carried in to the fire, the unclothed and modest Hamblin remained on the platform of logs. In spite of the tortures of the chill morning air, he refused to go inside until George Young, the Ohio trooper with the scalded hand, came to his rescue. Stepping out of the cabin and seeing Hamblin—"a one-armed comrade, entirely naked, poor from a long prison life and shivering in the wind"—Young pulled off his drawers, slipped into the trousers he had picked up in the river and gave the drawers to Hamblin. With the baggy underwear clutched about his wasted buttocks, Hamblin was now willing to venture into the presence of the ladies.

A mile below Mound City, pacing the cypress log with his switch-marked companion, Captain Elliott watched the sky take on a leaden cast and saw the black, swirling Mississippi turn yellow-brown in the first light of dawn. Up and down the river, in both directions, he could see men perched on snags, standing on brush piles and clinging to treetops. A hundred yards upstream were six men on the roof of a barn—Brady, Ettleman, Gamble, Karns and the two others—the only successful riders of the gangplank. Just beyond the barn, through the morning mist that rose from the water, the captain watched a young soldier swim out of the stream and pull himself onto a drift.

The youth had been scalded so badly that his skin hung in strips. "Boys," he said, "it is going to kill me." A moment later he was dead.

Elliott was soon watching a different drama: forty yards from him on the riverside was a man clinging to a pole worn smooth by the waters. When the captain first saw him, his feet were above the water, and he was climbing with all the strength he had to reach a projecting snag where he could rest. Failing, he stopped, then slipped gradually, inch by inch, down the pole, until his feet were beneath the water. Again he tried to reach the rest, but he fell short of the point he had reached before. So periodically climbing and falling back, each time he sank lower and failed to climb as high as before. At last he had to throw his head back to keep his chin above the water, and when he climbed he failed to get his waist out of the flood.

As the man was about to make what Elliott was sure would be his last futile effort, the hard-working Rebel lieutenant, Frank Barkton, poled out of the brush. Shouting to him, Elliott pointed out the man on the pole. With considerable danger to himself, Barkton dragged the stiffened soldier into the canoe and put him onto the roof of the barn, where his comrades soon rubbed him back to life. For a half hour Barkton continued to dart back and forth, carrying others to places of safety. Then the *Jenny Lind* chugged up the bank and dropped anchor nearby. Barkton immediately began transferring survivors to the steamer, taking them from barn roof, drifts and treetops, working steadily until he finally picked up Elliott and his companion—the last two in sight.

Back at the Memphis water front, the *Bostonia* put her hundred survivors onto the wharf at the foot of Jefferson Street. While the unloading was in progress, someone on board noticed a soldier and two little girls drifting downstream on a plank. A reporter for the Memphis *Bulletin,* watching from the landing, saw a rope thrown to the solidier from the main deck of the packet. Attempting to catch the rope, the children slipped out of the soldier's arms. With no thought of saving himself, the soldier at once began diving in a desperate effort to find the youngsters; both were swept away by the current. Too tired by his exertions to catch the rope, the soldier was sinking without a struggle when he was rescued by a skiff from the wharf.

As soon as the unloading of the *Bostonia* was completed, Captain Watson rushed back to the disaster scene. Among the second group of survivors brought aboard was W. A. Huld of the 64th Ohio. When three men made off with the hatch cover he had thrown into the river, Huld swam downstream unaided until he was almost exhausted. Then, by the light of the burning wreck, he saw a small cottonwood tree floating along with a man in its branches. Huld thought the man might be unconscious, but when he caught hold of the roots he found out differently.

"Get offa there," the man screamed. "This tree's only big enough for one man, and I can't swim a lick!"

"I only want to rest a minute," said Huld, "and then I'll surrender the tree to you."

Shrugging off his suspenders and removing his trousers, Huld let go of the tree and set out swimming again. After a long time he saw something in the water nearby. Stroking crosscurrent, he found that it was covered with pitch and gravel—a portion of the *Sultana's* hurricane deck. Huld was still clinging to this float when he was found by the *Bostonia's* yawl.

C. M. Nisley, the commissary sergeant, was picked up by the *Bostonia* on her second trip as was W. P. Madden of the 44th Ohio, who remembered with gratitude the work of William Rowberry, the *Sultana's* first mate: "It was he, with the aid of a skiff, conveyed us to the boat, and although wet and chilled, he did not cease his efforts in caring for others as long as there were any found needing assistance. Even on the boat, where hot coffee and fire were accessible, he looked not for his own comfort until all others were first served."

Nathan Wintrenger also came in for praise from his fellow survivors. The chief engineer left the boat with a shutter, but soon he came across an unclaimed foot-plank about thirty feet long and fifteen inches wide. Drifting downstream, he urged others to join him and by the time Lieutenant George McCord caught sight of the plank, it was a life preserver for ten or more persons. There was just enough buoyancy to keep all heads above water, but Wintrenger was skillfully managing his craft, encouraging his companions and, at the same time, maintaining a lookout for more passengers. McCord swam near, was welcomed, and held on with the others until daylight, when they were picked up by the steamer *Jenny Lind*.

Only one other *Sultana* officer could be counted among the survivors. George Clayton, the pilot, knowing better than anyone else aboard the direction of the current and the lay of the land, made his way with a minimum of difficulty to Island 42, where he was found uninjured. Wes Clemens, the assistant engineer, was also found on the same shore, but he had been flayed alive by escaping steam, and he died soon after entering a Memphis hospital.

After the *Sultana* settled to the bottom of the river, John Fogleman and his neighbors at Mound City began taking turns piloting their raft. By nine o'clock in the morning, thanks to their efforts, a considerable number of survivors—standing, squatting or sitting —were clustered about a fire which had been built near Fogleman's veranda. Inside the house lay the injured—suffering quietly or whimpering with pain— in the bedrooms, drawing room and hallways. Nathaniel Foglesong and his companions from the rudder and the wreckage were here, in addition to the thirty-seven who had been rescued from the hull of the steamer.

William Boor, who had leaped from the bow with five hundred others, was unconscious when one of the Fogleman party found him in the timber, separated him from his board and ferried him on the raft to Mound City. Dimly, Boor realized that he was stumbling about on dry land, and he caught onto a log fence. In spite of the morning sunlight, everything seemed dark and murky. "Go to the fire," said a woman's voice, and then the darkness became absolute. After a time Boor became aware that someone was washing his face, although he could not imagine why. Murmuring voices gradually grew more distinct and he opened his eyes. He was lying on the front lawn, near a crackling bonfire, and he worried over the fact that he had lost his bundle of clothing. A man handed him a bottle. Boor examined the contents by sight and smell and handed the bottle back. "I do not drink whiskey," he said—the first words he had spoken since being rescued.

More survivors arrived at Mound City as the raft plyed busily between the island of timber and the landing. DeWitt Clinton Spikes was brought in and anxiously asked through the crowd for the other members of his family. On the next trip the raft brought back the bodies of Elethia and Elizabeth Spikes, both drowned. For a few minutes the lad was wild with grief at the sight of his dead mother and sister. Then he pulled himself together and grimly asked Fogleman if he might be allowed to help on the raft. The plantation owner and his exhausted neighbors readily agreed, and young Spikes was later credited with saving thirty lives. His father, his brother, his other two sisters, and his cousin were never found.

During the night hours, when oarsmen groped their way along the lightless stream guided only by groans and wails, the search for survivors was slow—fatally slow. With the dawn, the skiffs and yawls skimmed more quickly over the water and in the warm morning sunshine even the cries for help—some of them at least—became more cheerful. Up and down the bank men could be heard slapping their chests and crowing like roosters, mocking the trill of birds and mimicking frogs. Others greeted the day and signaled their position to the rescue boats with tremulous choruses of

"Mister, Here's Your Mule"—a favorite song of the Western troops.

The *Pocahontas* patrolled the shores of the islands and the Arkansas bank, stopping at Mound City and at the woodyard, picking up more than one hundred and forty men—Captain A. C. Brown, whose friends at Cincinnati had wanted him to have a pleasant trip; Chester Berry, who had sung of the hour of prayer; S. F. Sanders and Epenetus McIntosh, the only Illinois men among the parolees; W. C. Porter, who had been forced out of the coalbin at Memphis; C. J. Lahue and William Peacock, who had been tumbled from the texas roof; Absalom Hatch, who had been run over while sleeping on the lines at the bow; William H. Norton, who had almost lost his life on the mooring ring; Simeon Chelf of the 6th Kentucky Cavalry and his friend A. M. Jacobs, who had traded Chelf a pole for a plank; William Fies, who had watched a crazed man drown himself; Otto Bardon and Fritz Sanders, who had held to a door, along with their friends from the hard-to-steer trunk; Hiram Allison, who had clung to the center of a horse trough—some of them unconscious, many of them injured, most of them naked, all of them suffering from shock and exposure.

One yawl-load included two of the civilian passengers—William Long, alive, and Mrs. Hoge, dead. W. N. Goodrich, the Michigan farm boy who had camped on a garbage dump at Decatur and had been captured at Athens, grinning with relief, was plucked from a willow, which he had reached with the help of a hardtack box. Sergeant Joseph Stevens, the Yorkshire-born Michigan Sharpshooter, and his friend

Charles Taber were removed, unconscious, from their bale of hay. Roused by the movement, Stevens felt his wet clothing and dazedly asked if it had been raining.

A soldier who regained consciousness in the cabin of the picket boat remembered it as a confusing but gladdening experience: "They poured whiskey down me, rolled and rubbed me, and finally brought me back to life. I was like the newborn babe, not a raveling of clothing upon me, in a place surrounded by persons whom I had never seen before, but I was happy as a lark to think I was rescued and saved."

The boatmen approached a bare figure in a tree—a sergeant from some Michigan regiment—who was whisking himself vigorously with a willow limb. "Bully, boys!" he greeted them. "Here's your mule! I couldn't have stood it five minutes longer! Lord, ain't the mosquitoes big!"

Joseph Norris of the 51st Ohio was found on a bush, peppered and punctured by the bites of buffalo gnats, wearing not a stitch of clothing. When he was brought aboard the *Pocahontas*, a Sister of Charity—there were several on the steamer—gave him a shirt, and a fireman gave him a pair of overalls, while a Negro waiter poured him a glass of "something that did not look or taste altogether like spring water." By the time he had downed a second glass of whiskey, Norris felt like eating breakfast, and he found it waiting on the kitchen table. "I had not eaten at a table for nearly four years and was rather awkward," he confessed, "but I got there just the same."

L. W. McCrory was lifted from his log, and he also

met the messmate who was dishing out hot sling unsparingly to the boys. McCrory tossed off his portion and decided that it was not enough. He stepped up to the bar, asked for brandy, and the bartender set out a bottle and a glass. McCrory called for a larger glass and was given a sizable beer tumbler. Filling it to the brim, he drained it at a single draught and offered to pay, but the bartender told him, "It's free to *Sultana* survivors." The prudent McCrory, still holding onto his iron-bound pocketbook, said, "When you dispose of it wholesale, you ought to charge something."

Against the *Pocahontas'* starboard bulkhead lay Daniel McLeod, Wes Clemens and others who were maimed and mangled. On the larboard side lay the dead. Occasionally a body was carried across the cabin—transferred from the living to the lifeless side. One of these unfortunates was Thomas Butler, a *Sultana* watchman, whose face and hands were horribly burned. Another man was "so badly scalded," a witness declared, "that his skin slipped off from the shoulders to the hands." Wrapped in cotton and soaked in oil, he paced the deck until a few moments before he died.

Captain Thomas Day of the steam ferry *Rosadella* sent his skiff into the flood-wood, and it brought back several survivors, along with a number of corpses. One of the dead wore a fine white shirt, marked "J. D. Fontaine, Dallas City, Illinois." Another had been so thoroughly stripped by steam that, in Day's words, "not the size of a half-a-dollar of skin was left on the whole body."

At midmorning, while the *Bostonia, Jenny Lind,*

Pocahontas and *Rosadella* were still nosing in and out along the banks, two more steamboats arrived at the disaster scene—the *Rose Hambleton,* upward bound from the Arkansas River, and the *Silver Spray,* downward bound from Cincinnati.

Near the head of the Mound City island, two fishermen in a rowboat hailed the *Rose Hambleton* and brought aboard the body of a handsome young woman, about five feet five inches tall, with long brown hair and blue eyes, wearing an expensive nightgown fastened by a breastpin of plain jet set in gold.

Among those picked up by the *Silver Spray* were Congressman-elect Snow; Perry Summerville, the young Indiana forager who had been blown overboard; Commodore Smith, who had helped throw the injured from the *Sultana's* main deck; M. H. Sprinkle and Billy Lockhart, who had performed the same hard service on the hurricane deck; M. C. White, who had lost his board to a berserker; William McFarland of the 42nd Indiana and the woman McFarland had seen dropping her baby from the cabin deck. Both mother and infant were alive and uninjured. White remembered the kindness of the packet's passengers and crew—how they hurried the survivors to the stove side, brought them hot drinks and wrapped them in bed clothing from the staterooms.

But there was one soldier who was not impressed by the *Silver Spray's* solicitude. The tall, intoxicated Tennessee trooper who had raised such a ruckus on the *Sultana's* hurricane deck was seated comfortably astride a log when the yawl rushed to his rescue. He asked how far it was to Memphis, and one of the oarsmen replied that it was about a mile. "Go to hell with your boat," roared the soldier. "If you couldn't come to help me before now, you'd better have stayed away." And so saying he slipped into the water and began swimming downstream.

According to McFarland, the seven-foot Tennesseean arrived at the landing before the *Silver Spray,* but he was still somewhat drunk even after his long swim and all the excitement of the night. Ushered from the wharf edge to a waiting hack, he refused to ride. In an effort to force him inside, several soldiers were knocked down and finally a six-man guard was detailed to march him up the street to the hospital.

All of Memphis, it seemed, was on the levee. An excited crowd had begun congregating soon after the first news of the disaster, and now the long wharf was thronged with the curious and the concerned. Dr. B. J. D. Irwin, the army's chief surgeon at Memphis, was in charge, performing energetically and efficiently. Blankets and buckets of hot coffee were on hand. The Christian Commission had obtained from the quartermaster's department a huge quantity of red cotton drawers and undershirts, which the Sisters of Charity distributed. Every ambulance and omnibus in the city was backed up to the landing, ready to rush the survivors to the six local hospitals, where emergency staffs were hard at work.

Many of the injured did not realize how badly they were hurt until they reached the wharf. Here, after being out of water for some time, their scalded flesh began to blister. Before C. S. Schmutz could be persuaded to enter an ambulance, he ran up and down to cool his burning body. Going against the wind he found some relief, but each time he turned downwind the pain swept over him in agonizing waves.

Suffering humanity—mutilated, burned, lacerated, bruised, broken and grieving—filled the wards and spilled out into the corridors at Adams, Overton, Washington, Gayoso, Webster and Officers' Hospitals.

At Adams Hospital, Surgeon J. M. Studley examined Daniel McLeod's broken ankles and told him that one of his legs—the right one, which had been shattered at Shiloh—could not be saved. McLeod was wheeled into the operating room, where he breathed deeply the sick-sweet smell of chloroform. Later he woke up feeling lighter and relieved.

The wife, now the widow, of Lieutenant Harvey Ennis had to be placed under heavy sedation at Gayoso Hospital, and she fell asleep begging for news of her lost husband, baby and sister.

Down on the wharf Captain Elliott met the younger Safford, who had been picked up by a boat from the *Essex*. The young man was looking for his father, the Christian Commissioner, and Elliott helped him open more than a hundred coffins—the pine boxes being stretched out in a steadily lengthening single file. Failing in their grim quest, the two men visited the office of a local newspaper. Here they learned that the elder Safford had been found, unconscious but alive, on the shore of President's Island. And to the newsman who was compiling a list of survivors, Elliott revealed his true identity for the first time since being captured at Nashville four months earlier.

Late in the morning Captain Parker, now back aboard the *Essex,* organized searching parties and sent out ten small boats to cover both banks of the river for several miles, both upstream and down. Men and women were found floating stiff and lifeless with boards still wedged under their arms, or holding desperately in death to a treetop. Parker commented sadly that if the disaster had only occurred a few hours later, after daybreak, the naval force could have saved several hundred lives, instead of a few score.

By early afternoon the steamers had abandoned the search for survivors and the small-boat crews had turned their attention to recovering the dead. Scattered bits of human debris were gathered up—ugly fragments of bodies which had been torn to pieces by the explosion.

Memphis had been witness, or near witness, to dozens of steamboat tragedies over the years, and because of the kind treatment which its citizens had always given to the victims of these disasters, the community on the bluff had long since earned the sobriquet of "Good Samaritan City." Now the name was earned anew.

The crew of the *Essex* contributed a thousand dollars as a gift of sympathy for Mrs. Ennis, and the Chicago Opera Troupe scheduled a benefit performance for the *Sultana* survivors at Atheneum Hall. Sailors can be expected to care for their own, and theatrical companies often give of their talent, but the outpouring of charity that came from the people of Memphis themselves provided eloquent and un-

usual evidence of their humanity. The *Sultana* parolees were, after all, enemy soldiers in an occupied
land.

Merchants of the city generously responded to the
Christian Commission's appeal for clothing, and several wagonloads of wearing apparel of all kinds were
collected and taken to the Soldiers' Home. These same
merchants also stopped many survivors on the streets
and clothed them on the spot.

Truman Smith started walking uptown in underwear provided by the Sisters of Charity. "But at the
first block I came to," he wrote, "there was a great
crowd, and they wanted to know if I was on the boat.
I said yes, and they gave me a suit of clothes and
thirteen dollars in money."

Nathan S. Williams of the 5th Indiana Cavalry rode
to the Soldiers' Home, drank a cup of coffee and wrote
a letter home. Then he set out to visit the hospitals
in search of his friends. "I must have made a fine
show," he wrote, "with nothing on but a shirt and
drawers, bareheaded and barefooted. I did not go very
far in this manner before a clothier called me in and
gave me a fair suit of clothes."

Although the hospitals and the Soldiers' Home did
their best to accommodate all of the survivors, there
were not enough beds to go around, and many were
forced to sleep on the floor. At the Soldiers' Home,
Simeon Chelf and Abraham Rhodes spread newspapers before lying down, in order to keep their new
clothes clean. When the townspeople learned of this
situation, some of the soldiers were invited into pri-

vate homes, and several of the injured Yankees spent weeks-long periods of convalescence with hospitable Southern families.

A number of benevolent ladies hurried to the hospital room occupied by Mrs. Ennis, and this widow of a Federal naval lieutenant was soon surrounded by flowers and supplied with many small feminine luxuries.

Mrs. Carlisle, a local resident, was afraid that the dead women, including Elethia and Elizabeth Spikes, brought down by the *Pocahontas* and the *Rose Hambleton* would not receive proper treatment, and she had the corpses taken to her home on Dunlap Street. Here they were prepared for burial. Upon examination it was found that the woman with the jet breast pin had carried several letters with her; she was the pretty Mrs. Sally B. Woolfolk of Hickman, Kentucky. Her body was placed in a funeral vault to await the arrival of her husband. The two Spikes women were interred at Elmwood Cemetery on the day following their death.

Not everyone at Memphis found it easy to put aside the passions of war and forget the bitterness of defeat. While the bedraggled survivors were coming onto the wharf at the foot of Jefferson Street, one woman declared herself very much pleased at the sight. She was immediately placed in custody by the troops and marched off to Irving Block, where the city jail was located. "Such talk as this is the most extreme folly," commented the Memphis *Bulletin*, "and a person who could allow his or her feelings to become worked up to such a terrible pitch as to lose all feelings of humanity must be depraved indeed."

There was at least one other bad Samaritan in the city. Seth W. Hardin, Jr., the Chicago banker who had lost his bride, had also lost his trunk and several thousand dollars. Poorly clad in borrowed clothing, he sought accommodations at a second-rate boarding-house on Adams Street, near the river. In spite of his explanations he was told, "Nobody who looks like you look can register without baggage or money."

Hardin next went to the Gayoso House, the city's leading hotel, where he received a cordial welcome. Shown to a comfortable room, he rested briefly and then hurried back to the water front. Late in the evening, with weary steps, he returned to his lonely quarters. Seating himself at the desk, he composed an advertisement for the local newspapers: "On the morning of the 27th inst., my wife, Mrs. S. W. Hardin, was lost by the burning of the steamer *Sultana*. I hereby offer a reward of $100 to any person who shall recover her body."

Down on the landing, however, little time was spent in mourning the dead and missing. Rivermen had come to expect an occasional explosion, burning or snagging. And sad though such an event might be, it could not be allowed to interfere with the turning of other paddle wheels.

In its "River News" column of Friday, April 28, the Memphis *Bulletin* reported: "The weather yesterday was pleasant, with a very light shower. Business on the levee was not very brisk. Crowds were collected on the wharf witnessing the arrivals of the ill-fated steamer *Sultana*." But on the evening of that same Friday, less than forty-eight hours after the explosion, another crowd collected on the wharf, to laugh and not to cry. On Saturday the "River News" writer declared: "A good representation of the youth and beauty of Memphis gathered together on the steamer *Bostonia* last night, by invitation of Captain Watson, and, as we were informed, had a gay and festive time, which they kept up until the wee hours of this morning."

Other areas of the nation, enthralled by the climactic events of a four-year war and preoccupied with the recent assassination and its aftermath, paid even less attention to the *Sultana*'s tragic toll. On the fatal Thursday morning when the Mississippi River became thick-strewn with the quick and the dead, the public eye was fastened on the bodies of two men—Abraham Lincoln and John Wilkes Booth. The presidential funeral train was winding its slow way from Buffalo, where three thousand an hour had passed the coffin in single file, to Cleveland, where an open pagoda had been built in the city park to accommodate a double line. And at Washington, on the deck of the monitor *Montauk*, lay John Wilkes Booth with a bullet hole in his head, shot down in a blazing Virginia barn the morning before. Because of the lives and deaths of these two men—one supreme in fame, the other in infamy—the Memphis wharf groaned unnoticed under its long rank of anonymous cadavers.

By week's end the *Sultana* survivors were clamoring to be sent home, eager to complete the journey that had been so violently interrupted, anxious to tell their story to friends and family. Captain Elliott volunteered to gather them up and take them to Camp Chase, near Columbus, Ohio. Touring the hospitals on Saturday, he told all of those who were well enough to travel to report at the Soldiers' Home for supper.

After an early evening meal, outfitted with new uniforms, the men marched down to the wharf and climbed aboard the *Belle of St. Louis*, bound for Cairo. Their number was about two hundred and fifty, and a dozen or more, while insisting that they were able to make the trip, were so badly scalded that they had to be laid inside the cabin and nursed by their comrades.

The packet departed shortly after nightfall. As she churned upriver the soldiers on deck fell silent, each with his own thoughts, each straining to catch a last glimpse of some particular landmark, locale or object which would be forever bound up in his most vivid memories—the Hen and Chickens Islands, the Mound City landing, the woodyard shanty, the Arkansas timber, the *Sultana's* jack staff standing lonely and erect. But in the darkness nothing was visible save the rippling water—and this was the thing that each remembered best.

It was a long, long night. "Some of the more timid were springing up at every little noise," remembered an Ohio trooper, "thinking there was going to be another explosion. At one time we supposed that they were having a race with another boat, and one comrade said if he had a gun he would shoot the captain."

Sunday afternoon brought the survivors to Cairo. Elliott arranged for the injured to be placed in local

hospitals for the night and led the remainder to an
army barracks. Early the next morning he secured
railroad cars, and the party set out for Mattoon, Illinois.

News of the train's departure from Cairo clicked
down the railway telegraph line, and the men pulled
into Mattoon, twenty-four hours later, to find that most
of the town's citizens had turned out to give them a
hero's welcome. As William Boor described the scene:
"The platform at the depot was crowded from one
end to the other with the citizens of Mattoon and sur-
rounding country, with baskets filled to overflowing
with everything you could think of to eat. As fast as
a basket was empty it was refilled, and after we had
eaten all we could, it seemed as though the baskets
hadn't been touched."

While the picnic was in progress, Elliott bargained
with the station master for the use of cars to continue
the journey, and had a difficult time. If Mattoon cars
were carried to Indianapolis, he was told, they might
be held for a debt owed by one road to the other. The
station master finally agreed to allow his cars to make
the trip, in exchange for Elliott's personal pledge that
they would be returned—a pledge which was subse-
quently honored without question by the authorities
at Indianapolis. Even after this problem was solved,
however, there proved to be a considerable delay before the cars could be made available.

In the interim, the people of Mattoon opened their
doors to the *Sultana* soldiers. In the evening a meeting
was held in a new, but as yet unoccupied, hotel. Chosen
orators spoke in rolling rhetoric of the victories these

visitors had won and of the sacrifices they had made. "But what was the nicest thing of all," wrote Boor, "there were about forty ladies, dressed in red, white and blue, that sang several patriotic songs." One of the songs was called, "Welcome Home, Dear Brothers," and commented Boor, "it seemed that we were."

At one o'clock in the morning the cars were ready. Not wanting to see Indiana outdone by Illinois, Elliott had wired ahead to the mayor of Terre Haute and to Governor Oliver P. Morton at Indianapolis, thus insuring that his charges would be royally received and cared for as they passed through his home state.

On Thursday, exactly one week after the *Sultana* disaster, the weary band reached Columbus. While they were marching in relaxed fashion through the streets of Ohio's capital city, on their way to nearby Camp Chase, a man in a boiled shirt asked Abraham Rhodes with obvious disapproval, "What regiment is this?"

"No regiment at all," replied Rhodes. "Just a detail of Wilson's cavalry sent down the Mississippi River to catch alligators."

Back at Memphis, the remaining survivors were left to their own devices. "After being in the hospital a few days," wrote William McFarland, "I made my escape, determined to reach home as soon as possible. The first boat that came along was the *St. Patrick,* a handsome steamer plying between Cincinnati and Memphis. Like a burnt child dreading the fire, I dreaded getting on a steamboat. Adopting what I supposed was the safest plan, I crawled into the yawl hanging over the stern of the boat—as all side-wheel packets have—and never left my quarters until I arrived at the wharf at Evansville. It rained most all the way up, but I stuck it through. Every time the boat would escape steam or blow the whistle I prepared to jump, supposing the explosion was about to take place."

Many of the survivors were so fearful of steamboat travel that they at first refused to leave Memphis by way of the river, preferring to wait for rail transportation. But no northbound trains were scheduled for several weeks, and during that time most of the men gradually trickled down to the wharf and were carried away by the passing packets—some departing on the *Belle Memphis,* Captain Cass Mason's old command.

Seth Hardin, as he continued the search for his bride's body, was soon joined by others whose relatives or friends were numbered among the missing. At his sister Rowena's frantic urging, Captain Francis Dozier hurried to Memphis on the *Marble City,* accompanied by William Thornburg, one of the *Sultana* shareholders, and William D. Shank, a representative of Nanson, Dameron and Company, the lost boat's principal owner. John T. Mason, brother of Cass, also arrived by steamer from St. Louis, along with Z. C. Ingram, father of the missing pilot.

A tugboat, the *Little Giant,* was placed at the disposal of this anxious party by Captain Curtis, and together with a few others they set out for the wreck on the morning of May 1. With the flood waters receding, a portion of the hulk's forward deck now jutted above the surface. Swinging in close and tying up to the jack staff, the searchers surveyed the appalling pile of debris—bones burned to crispness, bits of charred clothing, a shoe containing the cindered remains of a foot, blackened skulls and limbs. Ingram, an elderly man, sobbed uncontrollably at the sight.

Rewards were offered—two hundred dollars for the body of Mason, one hundred for Ingram, one hundred for each of the clerks—and the searchers made other trips up and down the river. But their efforts were in vain, and within a week all returned to St. Louis. Francis Dozier sadly told Rowena that her husband could not be found, and she was left to grow old alone. Never remarrying, she outlived all of her eight brothers and sisters, dying in 1918 at the age of seventy-six and leaving a large bequest to establish a home for crippled children.

None of the dead officers were found except George Slater, the assistant steward. His body was recovered from the shore of an island above Memphis and brought back to the city. The local stewards' association bought him a fine coffin, provided a plot in Elmwood Cemetery and made sure that his funeral was well attended.

The other remains which were gathered out of the river received more summary treatment. Most, of necessity, were buried in unmarked graves at the Soldiers' Cemetery—a dark-complected man wearing a horsehair bracelet on his left wrist; a thin-faced, blue-eyed youngster who had stripped to swim; a red-headed private with an eagle tattooed on one arm. In a creaking, mule-drawn wagon they took their last ride through the streets of Memphis, stacked in rough pine boxes one upon another, unnoticed by the passing throng.

For over a month the Mississippi continued to yield a ghastly harvest of disfigured, bloated bodies. By the dozens they rose each night in the vicinity of the wreck, to bob and turn and drift silently away. Many were picked up by the *Jenny Lind* and the *Rosadella*, which made daily, barge-loading excursions. Others were sighted, and some were recovered, at Memphis, Fort Pickering and Helena. As time went on the decomposing corpses became an unspeakable, sickening horror. Upward-bound packets reported seeing them floating in the river, lying on the banks or lodged in the driftwood all the way to Vicksburg. And not a few, according to white-faced witnesses, were seen in the company of hogs and crows.

Meanwhile, Major General Cadwallader C. Washburn, commanding the District of West Tennessee, fired off a telegram to Washington. Addressed to the Honorable E. M. Stanton, Secretary of War, it read: "Will you please order an inquiry to be made at Vicksburg to ascertain why 2,000 released Federal prisoners were crowded on board the ill-fated steamer *Sultana,* against the remonstrance of the captain of the boat and when two other large steamers were in port at the same time, bound upriver, with very few passengers? The loss of life is known to exceed 1,400."

VII

The Old
Army Game

One of early America's favorite pastimes was a card game called "bluff." It was the simplest and purest form of poker. Each player received five cards, with no draw, and putting up the ante was the unpleasant responsibility of the dealer. Immediately after the distribution of cards the dealer handed a marker—usually a buckhorn—to the player on his left. And at the beginning of the next hand this second player was obliged to ante the specified amount. So the man who stood to lose was the man who held the buckhorn, and he was understandably anxious to pass it along. During the Civil War this game—sometimes known as passing the buck—became very popular in the army.

Cadwallader C. Washburn broke the seal on a new deck of cards when he dispatched his telegram to Washington, and the ante was very likely to be someone's scalp.

Edwin M. Stanton, the Secretary of War, a paunchy autocrat with muttonchop whiskers, sent the questioning message along to Major General E. A. Hitchcock, Commissioner for Exchange of Prisoners, and indicated that he wanted answers. Hitchcock promptly replied that he knew nothing about the affair except what he had read in the papers: ". . . it is impossible at the present time to indicate who, if anyone, is at fault."

Hitchcock, in turn, handed the buckhorn to Brigadier General William Hoffman, Commissary General of Prisoners. But Hoffman's assistant, Major G. Blagden, hastily explained: "The Commissary General of Prisoners has no control over the transportation of paroled prisoners from the place of delivery to the various parole camps, the matter being entirely under the direction of the department commander who receives them."

Thus, within the brief span of three days, the buck was passed from Stanton to Hitchcock to Hoffman to Major General N. J. T. Dana, commanding the Department of Mississippi—and the game was still young.

On April 30 Hitchcock ordered Hoffman to proceed to Memphis and Vicksburg, "to inquire into the circumstances of the destruction of the steamer *Sultana* in the Mississippi River." Specifically, Hoffman was expected to find out how many men had been lost, what had caused the disaster and, most important of all, who was to blame.

Stopping briefly at Memphis during the first week in May, Hoffman learned that Washburn, on his own initiative, had convened a court of inquiry the day following the disaster; and when Hoffman arrived at Vicksburg, he found that a commission appointed by Dana was also conducting an independent investigation. Both of these hearings were completed by May 8, eleven days after the *Sultana* explosion, at which time Hoffman requested, and soon received, a complete transcript of each proceeding.

Hoffman then asked Dana to give him a detailed report of the events leading up to the *Sultana's* departure from Vicksburg. In response, Dana submitted a lengthy and surprisingly frank summary of his department's reception and shipment of the paroled prisoners. He recounted Williams' appointment as commissioner of exchange, the subsequent trip by Williams to Mobile and Cairo, Speed's voluntary assumption of responsibility, the charges of bribery and the loading of the packets. He added that at his headquarters office on the morning of April 25, a few hours after the *Sultana* left Vicksburg, he had been told by Speed that there were nineteen hundred men on the boat. "Having never seen the boat," wrote Dana, "I inquired as to her capacity and as to the comfort of the men, and was assured by both Captain Speed and Captain Williams that the load was not large for the boat; that the men were comfortable and not overcrowded, and that there were very few boats which had so much room for troops as the *Sultana*."

When Hoffman received this statement he noted that it was not militarily precise on the subject of responsibility. Because of Williams' departure and reappearance, the chain of command had developed a kink, and Hoffman wanted it straightened out. So he returned the report with a scribbled question: "Will General Dana please state what officer or officers he considers responsible for the shipment of the paroled troops within referred to, and for the proper character of the transportation?"

Dana replied: "Captain Speed was intrusted with the transfer and shipment of the prisoners, and assumed full and active management and control of it, and I therefore considered him fully responsible therefor. The quartermaster's department was ordered to provide the transportation, and I consider Captain Kerns, quartermaster in charge of transportation, responsible for the character of it."

In an effort to count the fatalities, Hoffman next asked the departmental commander for a list of the Federal soldiers who had embarked on the *Sultana*. Dana replied that he had no such list; all the reports and papers concerning the shipment had been lost with the *Sultana*. The only thing that Dana could offer was the Confederate roster of Indiana, Kentucky, Michigan, Ohio, Tennessee and Virginia prisoners who had been delivered at Camp Fisk. This he sent to Hoffman, along with the following notation: "The majority of the men named on the rolls transmitted herewith were on the *Sultana*. All such were originally checked thus (√), but since the shipment some names have been checked on the same rolls, so that it is impracticable at this time to identify the men who were on the *Sultana*. . . ."

Remaining at Vicksburg for a little more than a week, Hoffman conducted several interviews of his own. Then, his satchel bulging with material, he climbed aboard a train for the return trip. In Washington he found a crisp message from General Washburn, the West Tennessee commander at Memphis, dated May 14: "Twelve commissioned officers and 757 enlisted men make the total of paroled prisoners saved from the steamer *Sultana*." Adding this final bit of information to his collection, the commissary general of prisoners stacked the papers on his desktop, leaned back in his chair and surveyed the pile. Before him now rested all of the available facts and figures, opinions and allegations. Somewhere in this small mountain of words he would have to find, if he was to find them at all, the answers to those three questions: How many, what and who?

On May 19, after five days of shuffling the sheets and pondering the problems, Hoffman picked up his pen and wrote his report to Secretary of War Stanton.

At the outset he expressed his conviction that a wrong had been done: "Upon a careful consideration of all the facts as presented in the testimony herewith submitted, I am of the opinion that the shipment of so large a number of troops on one boat was, under the circumstances, unnecessary, unjustifiable, and a great outrage on the troops."

Putting first things first, he began by taking up the question of who was to blame: "A proper order was issued by the general commanding the department for the embarkation of the paroled prisoners, and there were four officers of his staff who were responsible that the order was properly carried out, *viz.*, Col. R. B. Hatch, captain in the quartermaster's department, chief quartermaster; Capt. Frederic Speed, assistant adjutant general, U. S. Volunteers, adjutant general Department of Mississippi; Capt. George A. Williams, First U. S. Infantry, commissary of musters and in charge of paroled prisoners; and Capt. W. F. Kerns, assistant quartermaster, U. S. Volunteers, and master of transportation. If there was anything deficient or unsuitable in the character of the transportation furnished, one or more of these officers should be held accountable for the neglect."

With these few deft strokes of his pen, Hoffman absolved Dana of any responsibility for the disaster. The "proper order" which he so readily approved was Dana's instruction to ship the paroled prisoners "about one thousand at a load." Hoffman saw nothing wrong with this order. Nor did he see anything wrong in the fact that Dana had personally visited the wharf and watched the *Henry Ames* depart with thirteen hundred men; nor in the fact that Dana had agreed to the placing of as many as fourteen hundred parolees on the *Sultana;* nor in the fact that Dana had made no effort to telegraph Helena or Memphis to have a part of the load removed when he learned from Speed shortly after the *Sultana* left Vicksburg that there were at least nineteen hundred men on board. None of these facts drew criticism or even comment from Hoffman as he took the buckhorn from Dana and prepared to hand it to one or more subordinates.

After describing the loading of the *Sultana,* Hoffman's report continued: "I am of the opinion that the four officers above-named are responsible for the embarkation of so large a number of troops on an unsuitable vessel, Colonel Hatch and Captain Speed being the most censurable. It was their duty especially to see that the service was properly performed. Captain Williams was assisting Captain Speed and seems to have felt that there was no special responsibility resting on him, but there was a manifest propriety in his knowing the number embarked, and if there was a deficiency of transportation he should have reported it. Captain Kerns made no inspection of the steamer to see that she was properly fitted up, but he did report her to Colonel Hatch, and also to General Smith, as being insufficient for so many troops, and his report should have been noticed. He made no report of the repairing of the boilers, which he seems to have been aware was going forward, and which it has not yet been decided positively was not the cause of the disaster. Lieut. W. H. Tillinghast, Sixty-sixth U. S. Colored Infantry, was the only other officer connected with this service, but he had no directing control. It is shown by his own testimony that a bribe was profferred to him to induce him to use his influence in having some of the troops shipped on the *Pauline Carroll,* which he showed a willingness to accept—at least he did not reject it—and which he failed to report until after the loss of the *Sultana.*"

So there had been skulduggery afoot. Tillinghast had been offered a bribe, apparently by the Vicksburg agent of the Atlantic and Mississippi Steamship Company. But in all of the testimony taken during the Vicksburg inquiry—and the agent himself was called as a witness—this was the only evidence of attempted bribery uncovered. It seems obvious that if the agent had been dealing with Hatch, Speed, Williams or Kerns, or if he had thought it possible to make an illegal arrangement with any of these men in authority, he would not have approached the unimportant Tillinghast. The offer to Tillinghast, then, was the tiny fire which had raised such a blinding smoke of suspicion—a fire which Dana might easily have stamped out, if he had only taken the trouble to investigate the gossip.

Hoffman added: "The testimony of the four officers above referred to"—Hatch, Speed, Williams and Kerns —"is very contradictory, and I have formed my opinion from the general tenor of the testimony and the circumstances of the embarkation. Brig. Gen. M. L. Smith, U. S. Volunteers, had command of the District of Vicksburg at the time, but he had nothing officially to do with the shipment of the troops; yet as it was officially reported to him by Captain Kerns that too many men were being put in the *Sultana,* it was proper that he should have satisfied himself from good authority whether there was sufficient grounds for the report, and if he found it so he should have interfered to have the evil remedied. Had he done so the lives of many men would have been saved."

Thus, with a few chiding remarks for Williams, Kerns, Tillinghast and Smith, the buckhorn was passed to Hatch and Speed. In making this assessment of blame among Dana's subordinates, Hoffman appears to have been on solid ground. As he pointed out, Smith had had nothing officially to do with the shipment; Tillinghast had had no directing control; and Kerns had reported the overloading to his superior, Colonel Hatch, who had refused to take any action.

The only difficulty came in unkinking the chain of command—in deciding whether Speed or Williams had actually been in charge of the loading. Here Hoffman was obviously guided by Dana's unequivocal statement: "Captain Speed was intrusted with the transfer and shipment of the prisoners, and assumed full and active management and control of it, and I therefore considered him fully responsible therefor." In addition, Speed had held the position of adjutant general of the department and was presumed to speak for the commanding general in all matters. For this reason, if for no other, Speed's orders could not have been resisted by Williams. Hence, Hoffman drew a conclusion which was altogether justified, and indeed was inescapable: "Captain Williams was assisting Captain Speed."

Next, Hoffman turned to the question of what had caused the explosion, and he frankly admitted his inability to find the answer: "In reference to the immediate cause of the calamity, the testimony which I have been able to collect does not enable me to form a positive opinion. The testimony of the two engineers of the *Sultana* and of the inspector at Saint Louis establishes that her boilers were in good condition on her leaving that port for New Orleans, and apparently continued so until her arrival within ten hours' run of Vicksburg, when a leak occurred in one of her boilers. On the arrival of the boat at Vicksburg, this leak was repaired by a competent boilermaker, and was pronounced by him a good job, though he qualifies the character of the work by saying that to have been thorough and permanent the two sheets adjoining the leak should have been taken out, and that in its then condition it was not perfect. The first engineer, Mr. Wintrenger, testifies that after leaving Vicksburg he watched the repaired part of the boiler, which was near the front end, just over the fire bars, carefully, and it did not at any time show the least sign of giving way. When he was relieved from charge of the engine by the second engineer, the boilers were full of water and in good condition, and on their return to Memphis the second engineer, Mr. Clemens, who, being on watch at the time of the explosion, was fatally scalded, told him before he died that the boilers were all right and full of water. I was told by another engineer at Cincinnati that he [Clemens] had said the same thing to another person on landing at Memphis, but this other person was not within my reach. There is nothing to show that there was any careening of the boat at the time of the disaster, or that she was running fast. A piece of boiler was obtained from the wreck, by order of General Washburn, which I examined. It seemed to have been broken from the bottom of the boiler the breadth of a sheet and torn tapering to near the top of the boiler, tearing the iron like paper, at times through the rivet holes and then through the middle of the sheet. The lower or wider end seems to have been exposed to the fire without the protection of water, and if so, this doubtless was the cause of the explosion. But this piece of iron may have been exposed to the fire of the burning vessel after the explosion, in which case some other cause must be found to account for it. The testimony of some of the most experienced engineers on the Western rivers is given, to throw some light on the matter, but until the boilers can all be examined no reliable conjecture can be made to account for the explosion. Thus far nothing has been discovered to show that the disaster was attributable to the imperfect patching."

In plain truth, the whole subject of compression mechanics was, at this time, mysterious and misunderstood. Steam boilers were still new-fangled devices, and even the men who operated them were extraordinarily ignorant of their behavior. "It is the common opinion among engineers," reported Hoffman, "that an explosion of steam boilers is impossible when they have the proper quantity of water in them, but the boilers may burst from an over-pressure of steam when they are full of water, owing to some defective part of the iron, in which case there is generally no other harm done than giving way of the defective part and the consequent escape of steam."

In other words, most riverboat engineers were convinced that it was impossible to explode a boiler with anything less than runaway steam pressure. It was thought that even if the expanding gas developed enough force to break through a weak spot in the metal wall, only a harmless leakage would result. With a majority of engineers holding this naïve and dangerous belief, it is a matter of wonder that more steamboats did not blow up.

Contradicting this popular opinion, an engineer who was reputed to be "the most reliable on the river" told Hoffman that "the great power of steam, having once found a yielding place, tears everything before it, producing the effect of an explosion." Hoffman, who was astute enough to recognize the logic of this argument, commented that "his view seems to be reasonable."

Hoffman concluded his discussion of boilers with this observation: "What is usually understood as the explosion of a boiler is caused by the sudden development of an intense steam by the water coming to contact with red-hot iron, which produces an effect like the firing of gunpowder in a mine, and the destruction of the boilers and the boat which carries them is the consequence."

With the help of the dissident engineer, Hoffman had mentioned the two fundamental causes of most boiler explosions: First, the sudden development of runaway steam pressure by the water coming into contact with red-hot iron; and second, a normal pressure of steam acting on some weak or defective part of the metal.

It is probable that the *Sultana* was destroyed by one or the other, but which one is necessarily a matter of speculation.

Did Clemens let the water level fall below the safety mark, thereby allowing the upper firewalls to become red-hot? In a dying statement the second engineer insisted that the boilers were full of water at the time of the explosion. He had the reputation of being a "sober and reliable" man, and it seems likely that his dying words were true.

Was the boat swaying so sharply that the water was rocked away from the upper firewalls? Hoffman reported: "There is nothing to show that there was any careening of the boat at the time of the disaster." Yet one of the survivors, C. S. Schmutz, who had run back and forth on the Memphis wharf to cool his burned body, later wrote: "A great many of the soldiers were on the upper decks, and as the boat came round a bend of the river it would careen, the water rushing to one side of the boilers, the others would become heated, and as the boat righted the water would rush to the heated boilers, thus causing the explosion."

Undoubtedly the vessel was wallowing more than usual, because of the unaccustomed weight on her upper decks and also because the boat lacked ballast after the sugar was unloaded at Memphis. But long side-to-side rolls or sustained fore-and-aft pitching which might have overheated the boiler walls would have been noticed by everyone on board. And not one of the survivors aside from Schmutz mentioned any such movement. On the contrary, George A. Clarkson of the 5th Michigan Cavalry, who was suffering from diarrhea, visited the stern of the boat shortly before the explosion; and returning to his sleeping place near the bow, as he later recalled, he spoke to the engineer and commented on how "nicely" the boat was going. It therefore seems likely that Hoffman, who had access to all of the testimony, was correct in this instance, and that Schmutz was merely expressing an idea that had been planted in his mind sometime after the fact.

A normal steam pressure, on the other hand, could have triggered the explosion in either of two ways— by exerting sufficient force on the surface of the water to break down a red-hot dry pocket somewhere in one of the tanks, or by bursting through a weak spot in one of the walls.

In his annual report for 1865, J. J. Witzig, Supervising Steamboat Inspector, Fourth District, with headquarters at St. Louis, called attention to one weak spot that did most certainly exist. He pointed out that the patch which was riveted onto one of the boilers at Vicksburg was only one-quarter of an inch thick, and he declared: "This was on the part of the engineer a gross violation of the law, the body of the boiler being made of iron $1\frac{7}{48}$ of one inch, and inspected, and the safety valves regulated for iron of that thickness, and the pressure allowed (145 pounds to the square inch) was the extreme limit. Had the boiler been inspected after the repairs, the pressure allowed by law would have been 100.43 pounds of working pressure per square inch, as prescribed for boilers 46 inches in diameter, made of iron ¼ inch thick. From Vicksburg to Memphis the *Sultana* traveled at her usual speed, which shows that the usual pressure of steam was used. The foregoing is sufficient to explain the cause or causes of the explosion."

Wintrenger, of course, must have known that he was violating the law when he agreed to the makeshift patching. But it should be remembered that he would have considered such a procedure perfectly safe if he shared the popular opinion regarding boilers. And who can say, with anything approaching certainty, that it was through the patch that the steam found its deadly release? Judging from past performance, there is no doubt whatever that the *Sultana's* boilers were honeycombed with dry pockets and marred by weak spots. On two previous trips, as well as the last, she had undergone emergency patching along the way.

The real cause of the explosion seems to lie in the type of boilers used, rather than in their operation or condition of repair. Inspector Witzig himself described them in these words: "Boilers of a construction not adapted to the water of the Mississippi River, the flues being set in zigzag, which makes them very difficult to clean; the rapid accumulation of sediment renders them easily subject to be burned, or at least overheated; this seems to have been the case of the *Sultana.*"

Wintrenger, too, had long argued that the new marine fire-tube boilers were too easily clogged with silt, and for that reason were unsuited to use on the Lower Mississippi. This contention was apparently borne out by the subsequent loss of two other steamers with similar equipment. The *Walter R. Carter* went to pieces before the end of 1865, taking eighteen lives, and the *Missouri* let go the next year, killing seven. Following this pair of explosions, which gave fresh insight into the reasons for the *Sultana* disaster, the new-style boilers were removed from every packet that traveled south of Cairo.

Naturally enough there was unofficial talk of sabotage. Most of the survivors knew little about steam-boats or boilers, but they had a staunch faith in Confederate perfidy, born of war, nurtured in prisoner-of-war stockades and strengthened by the recent assassination of Lincoln. In spite of the fact that no proof existed, many of the parolees immediately jumped to the conclusion that Rebel explosives had caused the sinking.

Inevitably, the idea was adopted by the usual weird assortment of cranks and publicity seekers. In 1888, a resident of St. Louis, William Streeter, announced to a newspaper reporter that the calamity had been the work of a celebrated Confederate blockade runner and mail carrier named Robert Lowden, alias Charles Dale, who had wrapped a bomb in blackened burlap and slipped it into the boat's bunkers at the Wolf River yard. This bit of information, Streeter said, had been imparted to him by Lowden himself, just after the war. Lowden, at the time, was safely in his grave and unable to answer the charge. A few years later a Southern veteran "confessed" that he, not Lowden, was actually the guilty party, and that the torpedo had really been concealed inside a hollowed-out lump of coal.

It is safe to assume, however, that Hoffman and the other Federal officers would have liked nothing better than to blame the disaster on the Confederacy if they could have found the slightest shred of evidence to support the charge. Yet none of the testimony contains any mention of the rumor, and none of the investigating authorities even hinted at the possibility of enemy involvement.

Having dealt with the problems of fixing the responsibility and determining the cause—finding one confusing and the other insoluble—Hoffman devoted the last paragraph of his report to counting the casualties, with predictable results: "The reports and testimony show that there were 1,866 troops on board the boat, including 33 paroled officers, 1 officer who had resigned, and the captain in charge of the guard. Of these, 765, including 16 officers, were saved, and 1,101, including 19 officers, were lost. There were 70 cabin passengers and 85 crew on board, of whom some 12 to 18 were saved, giving a loss of 137, making the total loss 1,238."

Whoever and whatever was to blame for the disaster, the army was anxious to minimize the loss of life. It was plainly with this anxiety uppermost in his mind that Hoffman set the death toll at 1,238—a figure so low that it is little short of absurd.

The commissary general declared that there were 1,866 soldiers aboard the *Sultana,* and asserted that this figure represented a combined total of 35 officers and 1,831 enlisted men, including both paroled prisoners and the guard company. But in sworn testimony before the Memphis court of inquiry, both Clayton and Rowberry put the number of paroled prisoners alone, excluding officers and guard company, at 1,966. Congressman-elect Snow, who had examined the clerk's register before retiring, told a reporter for the Memphis *Argus:* "The bulk of the passengers were returned prisoners . . . They numbered 1,966 men and 36 officers." These two figures, added to the number of men in a full company under arms (198), makes a total of 2,200. And this is still 200 less than the troop total mentioned by the chief clerk in his conversation with Captain A. C. Brown: "He stated that there were 2,400 soldiers, 100 citizen passengers, and a crew of about eighty—in all over 2,500."

Hoffman reported that there were 70 cabin passengers and 85 crewmen aboard. Most steamboats carried about the same number of crewmen, which may explain why Hoffman gave the number accurately. But his pencil slipped again in recording the passenger load, which all of the witnesses agreed was approximately 100, not 70.

Assuming that there were 2,385 or more persons aboard the *Sultana* at the time of the explosion (2,200 troops and 185 civilians), and also assuming that 800 or less were saved, the total loss of life must have been at least 1,585. Probably this is a fair minimum estimate, although it is only that—an estimate. The United States Customs Service at Memphis recorded the number of deaths at 1,547. *Gould's History of River Navigation,* a respected contemporary source, made it 1,647. No one can say positively how many were aboard or how many died. Both military and nonmilitary survivors quickly scattered, singly and in groups, to homes and army posts throughout the Midwest. And many of the injured—more than 200 of them according to Memphis newspapers—were buried before the ink was dry on reports of their survival.

One thing seems certain and is agreed upon by most, if not all, who have made even a cursory examination of the facts: A combination of overloading and experimental boiler design had produced a catastrophe which still stands as the greatest marine disaster of all time.

When Hoffman's report found its way to the War Department and reached the desk of Secretary Stanton, the man with the muttonchop whiskers must have regarded it as a commendable piece of work. It was discreetly conservative in its estimate of casualties and satisfyingly vague on the matter of cause. But best of all it passed the buck to an insignificant colonel and a lowly captain of volunteers, which was much better than forcing the army to admit that one of its departmental commanders, a major general and a West Point man, had been caught napping.

In the turmoil and confusion that accompanied the end of the war, the old army game moved even more slowly than usual—which is to say that its progress was all but imperceptible. By the time Stanton finished shuffling the cards of justice, two of the players had left the table. First, on May 27, Major General N. J. T. Dana resigned his commission. Then, before the month ended, Colonel R. B. Hatch also slipped out of his uniform and into the safety and obscurity of mufti.

This left Captain Frederic Speed in sole and undisputed possession of the buckhorn. And as summer melted into autumn, he was called upon for the ante. On November 1, 1865, a general court-martial for the trial of Speed was convened by Paragraph 11, Special Orders Number 89, Department of Mississippi. The Charge was "Neglect of duty, to the prejudice of good order and military discipline."

Specification Number One alleged that the accused,

"being charged by Major General Dana, commanding Department of Mississippi, with the duty of receiving certain officers and men in the military service of the United States, paroled as prisoners of war by the Confederate authorities, and also being charged with the duty of superintending the transfer of said prisoners from Four Mile Bridge, near Vicksburg, to Camp Chase, Ohio, did neglect to avail himself of the services of *Col. R. B. Hatch, assistant quartermaster, chief quartermaster of Department of Mississippi, and* Capt. W. F. Kerns, assistant quartermaster, in charge of water transportation at Vicksburg, in procuring the necessary and safe transportation for the said paroled prisoners up the Mississippi River, but did himself assume to discharge the duties properly belonging to the aforesaid officers of the quartermaster's department by deciding and directing that a large detachment of said paroled prisoners, about 1,886 in number, should be transported northward in one steamer, the 'Sultana,' against the advice *and remonstrances* of the aforesaid officers, thus greatly overloading the said steamer, which on her trip up the river exploded, whereupon about 1,100 men lost their lives who would not have so lost their lives but for the misconduct of the accused. This at Vicksburg on or about the 23d, 24th, 25th, 26th, and 27th of April, 1865."

Specification Number Two alleged that the accused "did assume unwarrantable authority in directing the arrangements for the transportation of certain paroled prisoners, and did *without authority* load and cause to be loaded a large number, to wit, 1,886 paroled prisoners, on one boat, the steamer 'Sultana,' being largely in excess of the number she could safely carry, and when at the same time other *and better conditioned* boats were at the post of Vicksburg, ready and anxious to take a portion of said prisoners, the accused well knowing the same. And Captain Speed, *against the remonstrances of Captain Kerns, assistant quartermaster, against crowding so many men on one boat,* did with *criminal* neglect and carelessness cause the whole number, to wit, 1,886 prisoners, to be placed on the said steamer; and afterward *from the effects of which large load of paroled prisoners,* the boilers of the 'Sultana' exploded, whereby about 1,100 of said prisoners lost their lives."

The trial opened at Vicksburg on January 9, 1866, and ground tediously along for two months with the taking of testimony. Then the proceedings were prolonged for three months longer while a futile attempt was made to secure the presence of former colonel Hatch, who refused to answer three subpoenas.

At last, on June 5, a verdict was reached. Striking out the material printed in italics, the court found Speed guilty under both specifications of the charge and sentenced him to be dishonorably dismissed from the service. The proceedings, findings and sentence were approved by Major General Thomas J. Wood, who had succeeded Dana as commander of the Department of Mississippi, and the record was forwarded to Brigadier General Joseph Holt, the judge advocate general of the army, for final action.

During the second year of the war Congress had created the office of judge advocate general to serve as something of a military supreme court and to act as a clearing house for the army's increasing legal problems. At the time the legislative act was passed, Holt, a prominent Kentucky lawyer, former postmaster general and dedicated War Democrat, stood high on President Lincoln's obligation list because of his services in helping to keep Kentucky out of the Confederacy, and he had received the appointment as a political reward.

Originally, Holt's principal duty was that of reviewing, revising and recording the proceedings of all courts-martial, courts of inquiry and military commissions—no mean task, since a single war year might produce thirty thousand trials by courts-martial alone. Soon after his appointment, however, his powers grew far beyond even these considerable bounds. In Holt's hands the military commission became an efficient, inevasible machine of retribution, and he used it diligently—at times mercilessly—against secessionist sympathizers. The compassionate Lincoln, although he had seen the need for the machine, frequently interceded to commute capital sentences and reduce prison terms handed down by Holt's implacable tribunals.

After the President's death the broad, heavy face of Joseph Holt, with its bulb nose and deep-furrowed frown, became the visage of vengeance. With Stanton's co-operation, Holt disposed of the so-called Lincoln Conspirators in short order. Moving with suddenness and secrecy, he appointed a nine-man military commission which promptly convicted all eight defendants, the innocent along with the guilty, of conspiring to kill the commander in chief. Four were sentenced to long terms at Fort Jefferson Federal Prison in the Florida Keys, and the other four were hanged. Hardly had the echoes of this neck-snapping died away, before Holt had his hands on Major Henry Wirz, the former commandant at Andersonville. Although this dyspeptic little Rebel's greatest crime had been that of being in the wrong place at the wrong time, he too was promptly delivered to the noose. In both the Lincoln and Andersonville trials, Holt spared no effort to implicate Jefferson Davis. And though twice foiled in his attempt to execute the former Confederate President, the judge advocate was by no means ready to give up. Fourteen months after the war's end he was busy with new plans—which fortunately would never reach fruition—to try Davis and every member of his cabinet for treason.

On a day in mid-June, however, the press of routine duties forced Holt to put aside briefly his machinations and grandiose schemes. There were a number of courts-martial reports on his desk awaiting final action. One of them concerned a Captain Frederic Speed, the adjutant general at Vicksburg, who had been convicted of negligence in the *Sultana* case.

The judge advocate had a long-established reputation for damning with equal vigor the offenders of both blue and gray. Once he had approved and defended a court-martial sentence of five years at Fort Jefferson for a Union private who was guilty of nothing more than getting drunk and insulting an officer.

Now he flipped open a file and examined the record of an officer who was about to be dismissed from the service because he had caused or contributed to the death of some 1,500 of his fellow soldiers. It might be confidently expected that Holt would regard this proposed punishment as woefully inadequate and shamefully lenient. But not so. He regarded it as too severe!

In his report, dated June 21, the army's chief legal officer fumed at the injustice of Speed's conviction. Waggling an accusing finger at others in the case and chastising the members of the court-martial, he recommended that Secretary of War Stanton disapprove the sentence, which he referred to as "lifelong" and "terrible."

He declared that "Captain Speed took no such part in the transportation of the prisoners in question as should render him amenable to punishment; that his connection with the events which preceded the disaster to the *Sultana* was a wholly subordinate one; and that the facts developed in the evidence point out with distinctness other officers whose indifference to the comfort of those placed temporarily in their charge resulted in, though without causing, the death of over 1,100 of their number."

To support this contention he asserted "that the accused was appointed verbally by General Dana to act as commissioner of exchange during the temporary absence of Captain Williams; that Captain Williams returned the day before the men were sent to Vicksburg to go north, and that he immediately resumed the duties of his office." Further, wrote Holt, "Captain Williams, chief mustering officer on General Dana's staff, and commissioner of exchange, was present when the men were put on the *Sultana*, counted them as they went aboard, declared them to be comfortable, and insisted in a conversation with Captain Kerns that none should go on any other boat."

Then he hastened to add: "It is not the design of this report to cast censure upon the conduct of Captain Williams. He is shown to have been absent at the North until the day before the steamer *Sultana* sailed with her living freight, and cannot, therefore, be held responsible for the arrangements made before his return."

Holt berated Wintrenger for "criminality in risking the lives of so many men, knowing, as he did, the condition of his boat." But he found it "difficult to say upon whom the responsibility for the loss of 1,100 lives should really rest."

He thought that Hatch must have "felt a consciousness of some responsibility for the disaster" because he refused to appear at the court-martial. Yet he was not even sure that any crime had occurred at all, since "in shipments of troops by steamer no attention was ever paid throughout the war to the legal carrying capacity of the ship."

He stormed that the court-martial had "so emasculated the allegations of the charge as to absolve the accused of all responsibility for the catastrophe." And that, "Whoever should be regarded as meriting punishment for his connection with the event, it is believed that it is not Captain Speed."

Concluding this remarkable document—a classic of confusion and self-contradiction from beginning to end—the judge advocate wrote: "It is recommended that the sentence be disapproved and that Captain Speed be publicly exonerated from the charges which have been made against his character as an officer."

In view of Holt's previously demonstrated penchant for summary judgment and drastic punishment, his illogical but spirited defense of Speed was completely out of character. Perhaps someone pulled one of the myriad wires of Washington influence to have the convicted captain exonerated. More often than not throughout the war years and the reconstruction era, soldiers accused of everything from dereliction of duty to desertion could find official vindication if they knew the right people, or if they had friends or relatives close to high places.

It may be that Holt was merely helping to cover the last unsightly portion of a partially painted sepulcher. If this was his purpose, he accomplished it. With his defense of Speed, he applied the final brush strokes to one of the most effective whitewashings of all time. Dana had ordered, or acquiesced in, the loading of three steamboats with from three to four times their legal carrying capacity. Speed, with the active assist-ance of Williams, had exceeded even this limit in overloading the *Sultana*. Hatch had been informed of the overloading while it was in progress and had done nothing to stop it. Dana had learned of the overload-ing after the boat departed and had done nothing to correct it. Hundreds had died as a result of these blunders, yet everyone connected with the affair had been held innocent and blameless.

Without question or comment, Stanton followed Holt's recommendation, and on September 1, 1866,

Captain Frederic Speed was honorably mustered out of the service.

Now the buckhorn had passed full around the table —from Stanton to Hitchcock to Hoffman to Dana to Speed and back to Stanton again—and the game was ended. No voice was raised in protest. Few outside of the army knew or cared anything about it. Only a fleeting public glance was turned on the official investigations, while the court-martial itself was totally ignored. Not one single word concerning Speed's trial, conviction and exoneration appeared in the newspapers of Memphis, New Orleans or New York.

An orderly in Holt's office gathered up the leavings of the game, the great heap of records and reports, the mass of unwanted documents which chronicled the last voyage of the *Sultana*. He wrapped them neatly and tied them securely for delivery to the War Department Archives. On the outside of the package, as was customary in such cases, he scrawled the instructions, *For file—not to be re-opened.* But on this particular package a slightly different legend would have been more appropriate: *For file—not to be remembered.*

VIII

Historical
Amnesia

In the month of April, 1865, America provided the
setting for one of history's mightiest dramas. Its
players were the citizens of a divided, warring nation;
its stars were cast in roles of classic heroism and vil-
lainy; and its scenes tumbled after one another with
breathless rapidity. Robert E. Lee surrendered his army
to Ulysses S. Grant on the ninth day. Abraham Lincoln was shot in Ford's Theater on the fourteenth and
died the next morning. Joseph E. Johnston's surrender
to William T. Sherman on the twenty-sixth brought
the armed resistance of the Confederacy to an end.
Also on the twenty-sixth, the assassin, John Wilkes
Booth, died of gunshot wounds in a Virginia barn.
Such was the compelling power of these electrifying

acts that another—the agony of the *Sultana*—has been forgotten.

Certainly no other major event of the Civil War, and probably no other happening of equal significance in the whole colorful pageantry of the nation's past, is so little known.

The only comparable maritime disaster, the sinking of the British transatlantic liner *Titanic* in April, 1912, has inspired so many books, poems, plays, motion pictures and magazine articles that a *Bibliotheca Titanica* has been published. Yet at the present writing, aside from a collection of survivors' memoirs, not one single volume has ever been devoted to the story of the *Sultana,* which claimed more lives that the *Titanic*.

This strange case of historical amnesia is a malady of long standing. Even at Memphis, the city most concerned, reports of the tragedy were crowded out of local newspapers with remarkable abruptness. On the morning following the event, the *Argus* and the *Bulletin* each gave about half of Friday's front page to the details. (This was nearly all that the economics of the day would allow, since advertising was then carried on page one.) By Saturday, however, the *Argus* was again turning its attention to war news, and the *Sultana* was relegated to page two. Although the *Bulletin* featured the story for a second day, assigning a pair of its choicest columns to MORE ABOUT THE SULTANA EXPLOSION, it felt called upon to defend itself for doing so.

"Since publishing our yesterday's edition," the item began, "we have been enabled to collect a large number of additional incidents connected with the late terrible catastrophe occurring to the *Sultana*. Our readers shall have the benefit of our inquiries, as this is the most terrible and heartrending accident of the kind which has ever occurred in the history of marine intercourse.

"The celebrated *Dunkirk* floundering on the coast of England did not nearly come up to this affair in its terrible details of suffering. The *Dunkirk* was loaded with a party of excursionists amounting to about seven hundred and eighty. When well out to sea she struck upon a rock, not laid down in any chart, and was literally torn to fragments, and all on board perished. But that did not equal this calamity.

"The steamer *Pennsylvania,* on her way from New Orleans up the river, exploded her boilers when above Helena, about six years ago. This was one of the most terrible accidents ever before known. By this terrible catastrophe about three hundred and fifty persons were hurried into eternity. The whole country was startled and appalled by the horrible details of the *Pennsylvania* explosion. The press all over the country found food for their readers for many months, telling how it happened, who was on board, how they escaped, or how they sank to rise no more. Long legal investigation followed, and in fact the press had some new feature of the calamity to show up to their readers for weeks after the occurrence. Yet the waste of life by that unfortunate affair was nothing compared to the more recent case of the explosion on the *Sultana*."

In spite of this accurate appraisal of the story's importance, the *Bulletin* also fell unwilling victim to the deluge of other news, and in its very next issue managed to show up to its readers only enough new features of the calamity to fill about one-fourth of a column on page three.

On May 6, the *Argus* bestirred itself to lament: "We have, as a people, become so accustomed to supping of horrors during the past few years that they soon seem to lose their appalling features, and are forgotten. Only a few days ago fifteen hundred lives were sacrificed to fire and water, almost within sight of the city. Yet, even now, the disaster is scarcely mentioned —some new excitement has taken its place."

The New Orleans papers—*Picayune, Times* and *True-Delta*—contented themselves with reprinting articles from the *Argus* and the *Bulletin*. Thus when the story was abandoned at Memphis, it was abandoned at New Orleans as well.

On Saturday, April 29, two days after the explosion, the first brief dispatch on the event reached the seaboard and was printed on page four of the New York *Times,* under the headline, DREADFUL DISASTER. During the next four days the country's leading journal allotted a total of less than two columns to the story. Its last item on the subject appeared on Wednesday, May 3, and reported: "No troops belonging to States east of Ohio were lost." After this the *Times* lost interest and made no further mention of the affair.

Harper's Weekly, a pioneer news magazine, published a masterful woodcut depicting the steamer in flames, but offered no written report at all.

Veterans returning home with stories of their part in the great disaster were dumbfounded to discover that most people knew little or nothing about the event. Expecting exclamations of wonder and interest, they told their friends, "I was aboard the *Sultana*," only to be confronted by blank stares. And the hundreds who carried scars of the adventure were even more surprised when their applications for compensation were delayed by War Department clerks who had difficulty locating any record of the unheard-of Mississippi steamboat.

It was partly to further their claims for pensions, but mostly because of a desire to trade memories, that the survivors formed an association in later years.

A quarter century after their common ordeal, on Tuesday, April 29, 1890, they held a reunion at Adrian, Michigan, a conveniently located little town near the borders of Ohio and Indiana. Here came McCrory and Stevens, Raudebaugh and Horner, Sprinkle and Foglesong and some fifty others. But time had wrought its changes, and as they gathered in the crowded lobby of a local hotel, they were young troopers no longer, but middle-aged farmers, mechanics, brick masons, mail carriers, merchants, carriage trimmers, whipstock makers, miners and many other things.

In the evening, following a "grand campfire," they ate dinner together in the hotel dining room and all tried to talk at once—old soldiers renewing old acquaintances—describing the wives and numbering the children they had acquired, sitting at long linen-covered tables and smacking their lips (these men who had known what it meant to be hungry) over deviled eggs and baked ham, laughing in the promise of spring and the glow of camaraderie, recalling their night of horror with anecdotes that were more often merry than morose.

George Robinson, who was taking a few days off from clerking in an Owosso, Michigan, shoe store, remembered the man he had seen wrestling with a beer keg and praying with all his might. The man kept pleading with God and trying to climb on top of the keg, and the way Robinson told it: "He got up a little too far and over he went, still hanging to it. He came up on the other side of it and the first thing I heard him say was, 'Damn this thing, it'll drown me yet.'"

"Now, when I hear persons talking about being hard up," said A. C. Brown, a plump, fifty-one-year-old Georgetown, Ohio, shoemaker, "I think of my condition at that time—up in a tree in the middle of the Mississippi River, a thousand miles from home, not one cent to my name, nor a pocket to put it in. To contrast my appearance then, with my face scratched and swollen and my weight about one hundred pounds, with my appearance today reminds me of two Irishmen who, on meeting, each thought he recognized an old acquaintance, but they afterwards found they were mistaken. One said to the other: 'You thought it was me and I thought it was you, but bejabers it was neither of us!'"

J. Walter Elliott wanted to know if anybody had heard from George McCord. "I wonder," said Elliott, "if he ever laughs over my giving him my red flannel drawers and of his promenade with me through Memphis to the quartermaster's, barefoot and clad only in red shirt and drawers." Elliott's doctor had advised him to take his scalded lungs to a warmer climate, and he had settled a section of government land near Arab, Alabama. McCord had strayed even farther, moving west, serving for a time as sheriff of Marshall County, Iowa, and finally drifting all the way to Hanford, California, where he was employed as a bank teller.

One-time Cavalryman Truman Smith, now proud of his job as Captain of Number Five Steamer, Grand Rapids Fire Department, asked if anybody would admit being among the trio he had seen navigating a large tree downstream while loudly singing "The Star-Spangled Banner."

But despite the conviviality and good humor, no one could really forget the horror of the occurrence which had brought them here. The crashing roar of the explosion, the mangled bodies, the screams and moans of the terrified and trapped, the spreading flames, the stampede for the rail, the clutching mass at the bow and stern, the lonely darkness, the long hours in the frigid water, the pain of scalded flesh and the friends who were lost—of these things, too, they spoke, quietly and sometimes tearfully.

After the dinner there were speeches, of course. William Fies, now an undertaker, and Adjutant of the National *Sultana* Survivors' Association, offered a few remarks. Next came several sonorous, rolling orations by dignitaries from the county courthouse and the city hall, full of praise and patriotism, all punctuated by enthusiastic applause. Last of all, the association's newly elected major, Chester Berry, who was now a minister, pronounced a prayer for the absent and a benediction on those present. And then the neighborly visiting and story swapping spilled back into the lobby and continued until late into the night.

These men of the *Sultana* had played their exciting scene to a distracted, inattentive audience, and their bows had been taken before an empty house. Now even the supporting cast, the rivermen—the courtly captains, the daring pilots, the cursing mates, the sweating engineers and the carefree roustabouts—were quitting their roles. Even the props, the paddle-wheel steamboats—the romantic, racing Queens of the River —were leaving the stage. Marveling at these facts, the neglected players went home to watch the footlights dim with time and wait for the final curtain to fall.

It remained for the Old Man to add an epilogue. With specks of silt and grains of sand—depositing, smoothing, shifting, heaping—he softly covered the wreck of the *Sultana*, planted willows on the grave and moved away as if in shame. During the century that has passed since the boat went down, the restless Mississippi River has changed its course in the vicinity three times, and today it flows three miles east of the still-tiny community of Mound City.

In 1955, a West Memphis lumberman, A. P. Dacus, announced that he intended to dig for the remains, which he believed to be buried beneath his land. It was his hope that the hull could be restored and placed on public exhibition. Perhaps he was also intrigued by the thought of what might be found in the clerk's safe, and he probably wondered whether the Spikes family's seventeen thousand dollars in gold was still aboard. After a preliminary search with electronic metal detectors, he thought that the shattered boilers had been located, but he died before his plans for an excavation could be acted upon.

And so the corpse of the crumpled packet still lies somewhere under the fertile soil of the Arkansas flats, abandoned to the loneliness of obscurity. Writing of another steamboat which had suffered a like fate, Mark Twain made a prophecy which may yet be fulfilled by the lost *Sultana:* "Some farmer will turn up her bones with his plow one day, no doubt, and be surprised."

Author's Note

My interest in the *Sultana*—and in the multitude of Union soldiers who were aboard her when she exploded, burned and sank—had an early beginning since one of the blue-clad passengers was my grandfather, J. Walter Elliott, whose name I bear. Unlike the less fortunate majority, he lived to tell the tale. And though he died long before I was born, I often heard a secondhand recounting of his adventures from my father.

In 1956, I first began digging into the subject, intending only to write an article—one which appeared as a three-part serial in the Nashville *Banner*—but in the course of this ground-breaking research I became hopelessly involved. Beneath the surface, buried under the neglect of years and obscured by a unique combination of circumstances, was a singular human saga, waiting to be revealed.

Many individuals and institutions were kind enough to help in the spading and sifting. I am indebted, for generous assistance, to Mr. C. Moffett Moore, Chief Reference Librarian of the Memphis Public Library; Miss Ruth Ferris, Assistant Curator of the Missouri Historical Society's Mississippi River Collection; Mrs. Dorothy E. Powers, Curator of the Cincinnati Public Library's Inland Rivers Library; Miss Geneva Kebler, Archivist in Charge of the Michigan Historical Commission's archives; to the public libraries of Birmingham, Chicago, New Orleans, New York, St. Louis and Vicksburg; to the Library of Congress, the Steamship Historical Society of America, the Chicago Historical Society, the Ohio Historical Society, the Illinois State Historical Library, the Alabama Department of Archives and History, the Mississippi Department of Archives and History, the Louisiana Archives and Records Commission, the Vicksburg National Military Park, the Andersonville National Cemetery and Prison Park, the St. Louis *Post-Dispatch* and the St. Louis *Globe-Democrat;* and to three gentlemen who know all about steamboats—Mr. Leonard V. Huber of New Orleans, Dr. Walter E. Johnston of Vicksburg and Mr. Frederick Way, Jr. of Sewickley, Pennsylvania.

Throughout the book, I have frequently used the actual words of participants. All the dialogue is genuine, recorded by those who spoke it or heard it.

In the bibliography will be found a complete list of source materials. Each of these works made an invaluable contribution, and to each of their authors and editors I am sincerely grateful. Most of the first-person accounts by survivors were gathered by Chester Berry, and a few more were collected by Jesse Hawes for his excellent memoir of Castle Morgan. Without their timely efforts the most important part of the *Sultana* story—the flesh-and-blood part—would have been lost forever, and this book could not have been written.

Bibliography

BOOKS AND MAGAZINES

Berry, Chester D., *Loss of the Sultana and Reminiscences of Survivors*. Lansing, Michigan, Darius D. Thorp, 1892.

Bishop, Jim, *The Day Lincoln Was Shot*. New York, Harper and Brothers, 1955.

Catton, Bruce, *A Stillness at Appomattox*. Garden City, New York, Doubleday and Company, 1953.

———, *This Hallowed Ground*. Garden City, New York, Doubleday and Company, 1956.

Chipman, Norton Parker, *The Tragedy of Andersonville*. San Francisco, Blair-Murdock Printing Company, 1911.

Commager, Henry Steel (editor), *The Blue and the Gray* (2 volumes). Indianapolis and New York, The Bobbs-Merrill Company, 1950.

Durant, John and Alice, *Pictorial History of American Ships.* New York, A. S. Barnes and Company, 1953.

Gould, Emerson W., *Fifty Years on the Mississippi: Gould's History of River Navigation.* St. Louis, Nixon-Jones Printing Company, 1889.

Hawes, Jesse, *Cahaba: A Story of Captive Boys in Blue.* New York, Burr Printing House, 1888.

Huber, Leonard V., *Advertisements of Lower Mississippi River Steamboats.* New York, Steamship Historical Society of America, 1959.

——, "Heyday of the Floating Palace," *American Heritage.* New York, The American Heritage Publishing Company, October, 1957.

Isham, Asa B.; Davidson, Henry M.; and Furness, Henry B., *Prisoners of War and Military Prisons.* Cincinnati, Lyman and Cushing, 1890.

Lloyd, James T., *Lloyd's Steamboat Directory and Disasters on the Western Waters.* Cincinnati, J. T. Lloyd and Company, 1856.

McElroy, John, *Andersonville.* Toledo, Ohio, D. R. Locke, 1879.

——, *This Was Andersonville,* edited by Roy Meridith. New York, McDowell Obolensky, 1957.

Page, James Madison; and Haley, M. J., *The True Story of Andersonville Prison.* New York, Neale Publishing Company, 1908.

Ripley, Eliza, *Social Life in Old New Orleans.* New York, D. Appleton and Company, 1912.

Roscoe, Theodore, *The Web of Conspiracy.* Englewood Cliffs, New Jersey, Prentice-Hall, 1959.

Russell, William Howard, *My Diary North and South,* edited by Fletcher Pratt. New York, Harper and Brothers, 1954.

Samuel, Ray; Huber, Leonard V.; and Ogden, Warren C.,

Tales of the Mississippi. New York, Hastings House, 1955.

Sandburg, Carl, *Abraham Lincoln: The War Years* (4 volumes). New York, Harcourt, Brace and Company, 1939.

Saxon, Lyle, *Father Mississippi.* New York, The Century Company, 1927.

Spencer, Ambrose, *A Narrative of Andersonville.* New York, Harper and Brothers, 1866.

Twain, Mark, *Life on the Mississippi.* New York, Harper and Brothers, 1902.

Wiley, Bell Irvin, *The Life of Billy Yank.* Indianapolis and New York, The Bobbs-Merrill Company, 1951.

————, *The Life of Johnny Reb.* Indianapolis and New York, The Bobbs-Merrill Company, 1943.

Wyeth, John Allen. *Life of General Nathan Bedford Forrest.* New York, Harper and Brothers, 1899.

————, *That Devil Forrest.* New York, Harper and Brothers, 1959.

NEWSPAPERS

Adrian (Michigan) *Weekly Press,* May 2, 1890.

Chicago *Times,* May 1, 9, 1865.

Chicago *Tribune,* May 1, 1865.

Cincinnati *Daily Commercial,* February 4, 1863.

Memphis *Argus,* April 28 to May 28, 1865.

Memphis *Daily Bulletin,* April 28 to May 28, 1865.

Memphis *Commercial-Appeal,* June 9, 1955.

(St. Louis) Missouri *Republican,* April 29, May 1, 1865.

New Orleans *Times,* April 15, 19, 21, May 1, 3, 1865.

New Orleans *True-Delta,* April 21, May 2, 1865.

New York *Herald,* April 16, 1865.

New York *Times,* April 29 to May 3, 1865.

St. Louis *Globe-Democrat,* October 21, 1918.

U. S. GOVERNMENT PUBLICATIONS AND REFERENCE WORKS

Report of the Supervising Inspector of Steamboats, a part of the report of the Secretary of the Treasury on the state of the finances for the year 1865. House Executive Document Number 3, 39th Congress, 1st Session. Washington, D. C.: U. S. Government Printing Office, 1865.

The War of the Rebellion, Compillation of the Official Records (128 volumes). U. S. War Department. Washington, D. C.: U. S. Government Printing Office, 1880-1901.

Compton's Pictured Encyclopedia (15 volumes). Chicago: F. E. Compton and Company, 1936.

Dictionary of American Biography (14 volumes). New York: Charles Scribner's Sons, 1946.

Encyclopaedia Britannica (24 volumes). Chicago, London and Toronto: William Benton, 1959.

Index